Grace for the Good Girl holds up a mirror and shows me myself. It peels back the layers, and exposes a sputtering, floundering good girl who's struggling just to keep her head above the water. And then it throws a life raft, pointing the way to the rescue and restoration found only when I give up the striving in favor of receiving rest and peace from the One who gives both in abundance.

—Kristen Pittman

This book has been life-changing, a powerful message of freedom and deliverance and what it really means to rest in Christ. I wish I'd had it years ago. I laughed and cried and scribbled in the margins and reread entire sections. It will continue to be a go-to book for me, a beautifully written masterpiece that has redefined the way I see myself.

—Marian Vischer

In the midst of coping and living out my life without so much as a clue as to how to unravel the story, *Grace for the Good Girl* found me. With book in hand, I'm opening doors in my heart that hold stuff I thought I'd dealt with. I'm facing the Good Girl and looking her straight in the eye. But this time, I have a friend, a tribe.

—Stacey Thacker

Grace for the Good Girl was written for every Good Girl as well as every Not Quite Good Enough Girl. In luminous and engaging prose and a voice as vulnerable as it is relatable, Emily Freeman casts light on truths that were always right there, but that were buried deep under a piled-up heap of striving and self-judgment. I walked away from this book with a clearer understanding of who Christ already is *in me*, and that changes everything. . . . It makes me want to *really* live.

—Shannan Martin

I love it. I feel like I can hear Emily's precious voice in my ear, as if she were sitting on my back porch just chatting and sharing with me.

—Paige Knudsen

I used to think of myself as a wild child. After reading this book, I've seen that my hiding places are not so different from a good girl. We both feel inadequate unless we measure up, and we never measure up. We both struggle to see ourselves as Christ sees us, and we both desperately want to be loved . . . no matter the costs. The truth that is spoken about so eloquently and personably in this book is that we are free to stop striving and simply receive what has already been given. What has already been done, and who we already are—complete in Christ.

—Melissa Lewkowicz

Grace for the Good Girl is full of Spirit and truth. It's gentle and bold, tender and powerful.

—Holley Gerth

Being a good girl seems smart. It seems wise. It seems safe, But being a good girl comes with an unrelenting problem: the good girl can never be good enough. This book unpacks the myths of the try-hard life, exposing them for the enslaving traps they really are. Even with the myths exposed, the journey from the good girl's slavery to true freedom in Christ can be long and arduous. Emily's book is a good and reliable guide for the trip.

—Richella Parham

Emily,
    So I come into your book with all this mess, and you move me to tears and to hope, and you make me smile and you make me laugh, and sitting down with you in the middle of this insanity has been one of the best gifts I've ever been given.

—Kelly Sauer

Grace for the Good Girl shares beautiful truth in a loving and grace-filled way. Emily is genuine and true, a beautiful example of living a life of grace.

—Vicky Maness

Emily Freeman is one of those rare writers: profoundly biblical, lyrical, transparent—memorable. Her emancipating words on these pages offer the needed keys to all the good girls longing to take wing—and soar home to God's heart.

—Ann Voskamp, *New York Times* bestselling author of
One Thousand Gifts

grace for the
GOOD
GIRL

grace for the GOOD GIRL

letting go of the try-hard life

emily p. freeman

Revell

a division of Baker Publishing Group
Grand Rapids, Michigan

Published by Revell
a division of Baker Publishing Group
P.O. Box 6287, Grand Rapids, MI 49516-6287
www.revellbooks.com

Printed in the United States of America

Library of Congress Cataloging-in-Publication Data
Freeman, Emily P., 1977–
    Grace for the good girl : letting go of the try-hard life / Emily P. Freeman.
        p.   cm.
    Includes bibliographical references (p.   ).
    ISBN 978-0-8007-1984-5 (pbk.)
    1. Christian women—Religious life. 2. Grace (Theology). I. Title.
    BV4527.F74 2011
    248.8′43—dc23   2011017321

11   12   13   14   15   16. 17   7   6   5   4   3   2   1

For John,
who lives and breathes the mystery of
Christ in you, the hope of glory.

Amy,

I couldn't have asked for a better sister-in-law or friend. I love you very much. Hope you love this book! It's rocking my world!

Love,
Robin

contents

the hiding

The first time I heard Andrew Lloyd Webber's musical adaptation of *The Phantom of the Opera*, I was fourteen years old. My sister was in the marching band, and they chose to play a compilation from the musical at competition that year. It was, of course, instrumental only. The music needed no lyrics to captivate me. And so, when my English class traveled by train from Detroit to Toronto to see the musical live, you can imagine my excitement. I sat in that darkened theatre and was moved to tears more than once: the richness of the voices, the surprising melodies, and the emotional performances. It was breathtaking.

One of my favorite scenes was when the actors entered the masquerade ball. The colorful costumes, synchronized dancing, and powerful music painted an electric, imaginative scene. And those masks! Feathers and colorful fabrics covered faces disguised beyond recognition. Hiding never looked more beautiful.

While I've been writing this book for the better part of a year, this masquerade scene has often come to mind. In the musical, the hiding is regal and elegant. And there is an element of fun in that sort of hiding.

A few weeks ago, I left my three children with a babysitter while I went to run errands. When I arrived home, the babysitter flashed a playful smile and proclaimed she had no idea where the kids were. With a knowing glance, we loudly launched a conversation about what may have happened to them. Perhaps they left home to explore the world, fly to the moon, or join the circus. As we talked, we moved around the living room, lifting the obligatory pillow as if searching for them. We could hear their muffled giggles from behind the curtains. I knew they were about to burst.

I flung the heavy fabric aside and shouted in mock surprise, "There you are!" They proceeded to jump with glee and excitement, wondering if I really thought they had left home for clowns and rocket ships.

Such is the joy of hide-and-go-seek: the best part of hiding is being found.

That is something we know as kids, but we tend to forget it when we grow up. I've done a lot of hiding in my life, but maybe not the kind of hiding you might think. I'm not a fugitive hiding from the law or a runaway hiding from my troubles. I didn't spend high school hiding boyfriends from my parents or pot under my pillow. I've never had a secret abortion, an affair with a married man, or been drunk, high, or put in jail.

My hiding was so clever that I had everyone fooled, including myself. The masks I chose to hide behind were not obviously offensive. In so many ways, the life of this good girl mirrors that of the party guests at a masquerade ball. My masks were nice. They were lovely. They were bubbly and likeable and attractive. They were the masks of a good girl. Yet, I hid behind them.

We live and breathe and move on this terrestrial masquerade ball, longing to display the prettied up, exaggerated version of ourselves to everyone else. Behind my pretty masks, I was a worried, anxious wreck of a girl. I carried the weight of the world on my shoulders, as well as that of Mars, the moon, and half of Jupiter. Although I had accepted Jesus at age seven, I didn't know what it meant to walk with him. I spent most of my time stumbling behind him, just trying to catch up. Though my relationship with Jesus was very real and full of true faith, it was often too structured and boxed in. I really trusted him. I really prayed and knew he was with me. I was a genuine believer. I struggled in my faith, but I didn't have a compartment for that. I glazed over verses that didn't make sense and highlighted the ones that felt good. God didn't seem big enough to handle contradictions, neither the ones I saw in the world nor the ones I felt in my heart. I thought life with Jesus meant trying to become who he wanted me to be, but it always felt like something was missing.

I felt as if an invisible good girl was following me around wherever I went, showing up without permission to shame and blame and scold. She was omnipresent, like a pretty little goddess in a pink, shadowy corner. She embodied the good girl version of my current life stage and shamed me accordingly: good student, good leader, good wife, and good mom. She represented the girl I wanted to be but could never live up to. I constantly worried that my imperfect status would be discovered. I often experienced guilt but didn't know why. I felt the heavy weight of impossible expectations and had the insatiable desire to explain every mistake. My battle with shame was constant and hovering.

Instead of recognizing my own inadequacy as an opportunity to trust God, I hid those parts and adopted a bootstrap religion. I focused on the things I could handle, the things I excelled in, my disciplined life, and my unshakeable good mood.

These masks became so natural to me that I didn't even know they were masks. I thought they were just part of my face. I moved through life hiding behind the good and lived out the mess in secret. I taught people around me that I had no needs and then was secretly angry with them for believing me.

Somewhere along the way, I got the message that salvation is by faith alone but anything after that is faith plus my hard work and sweet disposition. I lived most of my life under a system I designed for myself and I labeled it The Gospel. As a good girl, every choice I made was dictated by a theology of self-sufficiency. Life was up to me, and I was prepared to get it right.

And then Jesus.

There isn't any other way to say it. Jesus makes it safe to walk out from under that system. We have a God who sees and cares and notices. He will not come undone. He remains un-overwhelmable.

The words in this book will paint the portrait of a good girl in hiding. Perhaps you will recognize your own masks, the ones you have worked on for years to carefully craft and design and perfect. Rest assured that paper face is not really yours. Behind the mask, you are just a woman who longs to believe that Jesus makes a difference, but you have had difficulty collecting the evidence of it in your own life. The true gospel really is good news. For you. Right now.

The cross gives us permission to sit down on the inside because we have a God who knows what he's doing. Allow him to look beyond the girl-made hiding places you have so carefully constructed. I know it goes against all the words the world says are admirable: self-reliant, capable, strong, and resilient. But I am in desperate need of a source outside of myself all the time. And so are you.

I believe women need to talk about the ways we hide, the longing to be known, the fear in the knowing. Beyond that, I believe in the life-giving power of story, in the beauty of vulnerability, and in the strength that is found in weakness. In order to explore the truth, we have to put words and images on those ingrained beliefs we have about God and what he expects of us. We have to expose the invisible expectations and desires we know are there but may not have words for yet. Let me give you the words. Let me offer my stories and the stories of women close to me. Perhaps they are your stories as well.

1

are you a good girl in hiding?

God hath given you one face, and you make yourselves
another.

—William Shakespeare, *Hamlet*

*M*ost of my Halloweens were spent in dark back
rooms with the shades pulled, vaguely lit by the
blue glow of the TV. We didn't trick-or-treat and we didn't
hand out candy. We didn't celebrate Halloween. Instead, we
hid.

But there was that one glorious Halloween when the rules
were mysteriously lifted and Mom allowed us to dress up and
trick-or-treat. I didn't know why that year was different, but I
knew better than to ask questions. My sister and I were giddy
with glee, and we bundled up against the October wind and
headed out as Barbies.

I had a mask with holes for eyes and nose and a tiny
tease of a slit at the mouth, just big enough to stick your
tongue through but not big enough to get it back out again.
I had to alternate between seeing and breathing because the

one-size-fits-no-one mask was too big. My sister tells me we fought over my mask that day, I think because the painted plastic hair was better on mine. I won the fight, but I'm not sure how. I probably cried.

I loved wearing that mask. It had a sparkly crown painted on top of long, wavy, bright yellow hair. It was lovely. But behind the mask, it was hot. And uncomfortable. And stinky. As much as I wanted to be Barbie, the truth was that I couldn't wait to take the mask off so I could breathe again.

Life behind a mask may feel right and may even be fun for a short time. After a while, though, recycled air becomes stale and the effort it takes to continue trying to be someone you aren't becomes a burden rather than a game. Only in returning home, taking off the mask, and being you again will you find relief.

Chances are, if you are a good girl like me, you can relate to the hiding. You may be hiding from something, hiding behind something, or simply *hiding something*. The concept of hiding isn't new. It started way back in the beginning, with an apple, a snake, a lie, and a fig leaf. The hiding has kept me silent in relationships when I could have spoken out. It has kept me paralyzed with fear and anxiety when I could have danced in freedom. And this prison of self-protection has kept me from receiving the boundless, unfathomable, gracious love of God.

Wanting to Be Her

My idea of who I should be is at war with who I am. I want to be perfect in every situation. I just do. I want to know what to do. I want to know how to do it right. And I want to do it. All. By. My. Big. Self. Not only do I want to do everything perfectly, I want to look perfect while I do it. I want to act perfect and sing perfect and have perfect teeth. I want to parent perfectly, to wife perfectly, and to have a clean house. All the time.

My solution to the disconnect between my perfect, imaginary self and my real-life self is to force life to look the way I want. Somehow. Anyhow. And so I work and I labor and I do the right thing. I stay strong when I feel weak and I fake happy when I want to cry because my ideal image has everything to do with put together and nothing to do with falling apart.

Because I care so much what you think, my hiding has everything to do with you. I desperately want to manage your opinion of me. Nearly everything I do is to convince you I am good. If I sense any hint of disbelief on your part that I am good, if it seems your opinion is other than what I wish it to be, it becomes my job to change your mind.

If you wonder what gives you the authority to define me, I will say it is *because you exist*. I must have worth, and it is up to you to give it to me. It doesn't matter who you are; I want you to like me and I will hide my real self—with all of my real problems and issues and fears— so you can see what I consider to be my best.

When you mix this disorder of mine with the fact that I am a believer in Jesus, things can get very confusing. We tend to call the unbelievers lost. But this Jesus believer is in hiding. Is my experience of life any better than theirs? Freedom and victory are tossed-around concepts that I say I believe. And in front of you I know how to renounce the fear. But when I'm alone, I drink it down in gulps and gasps, like a hopeless addict returning to her vice.

If my story were a planet, then your rejection of me would be my nuclear holocaust. This fear of rejection drives me hard, eating away at my courage. And so I am cautious in my love. I am timid in my faith. My life tells a small story. I long to be seen, but I feel safe when I'm invisible.

So I stay a good girl.

And I hide.

I hide behind my smile and my laid-back personality. I hide behind *fine* and *good*. I hide behind strong and responsible. I hide behind busy and comfortable and working hard toward

17

your expectations. And if I do not meet your expectations, I hide behind indifferent. And though the purpose of my mask is to fool you, don't be fooled.

The energy it takes to live for you is killing me—to see me through your eyes, to search for myself in your face, to be sure you are pleased as it regards me. I want you to always regard me.

Please, by all means, *regard me*. I beg you to see me, to notice my goodness, to ignore my failure, to be inspired by my beauty, to be captivated by my essence. I want my loveliness to overwhelm you such that you cannot catch your breath.

And then there is God.

I know God is big enough to redeem the unruly, the rejected, and the addict. I know about the God who reaches way down into the pit and the One whose love stretches to the heavens. But I fear he misses the details. What about the girl in the middle? I fear I fall through the cracks because my story draws no attention. I lack intrigue, drama, and interest. Can he see ordinary, unspectacular me?

I'm not sure, so I vow to do everything right: to be a good girl, a good Christian, a good wife, a good mom. I believe he will be more pleased with me, a girl who does it right, than he would be if I didn't. I try hard to measure up to what I believe are his expectations of me, and I imagine him standing blurry in the distance, watching.

I want to let go, rest, and believe, so that he can hold, refresh, and redeem. But what if I do and he doesn't? To read between the lines of faith is to see Jesus. But reading between the lines takes work and invisible trust and the disregard of feeling.

I *feel* fear. It washes over me with its lies and half-truths. The lies aren't blatant. They marry themselves with a little bit of truth so the distinction is blurry at best. And so I practice the presence of fear and refuse the presence of Jesus.

When you reject me, be it real or perceived, I ponder and defend inside my head. And the fear wins a little more of my heart until I discover I am stuck by it, unable to move beyond it. My fear becomes my truth, and if you try to convince me otherwise, I am convinced you just don't know. You are naïve and I am a realist. You are too simple and I am complicated. You are wrong and I am right.

I lived this toxic way for many years before I understood about The Rescue. I live it still, when I forget that I've been found. Even for those to whom truth has been revealed, fear can be a loud and abusive motivator.

Fear drives.
But Love leads.

God can do anything, you know—far more than you could ever imagine or guess or request in your wildest dreams! He does it not by pushing us around but by working within us, his Spirit deeply and gently within us. (Eph. 3:20 Message)

That invisible good girl pushes me around. Fear drives, pushing and shoving. Love leads, working deeply and gently within. As I risk exposure to receive this Love, I catch a glimpse of his goodness, I am inspired by his beauty, I am captivated by his essence. His loveliness overwhelms me such that I cannot catch my breath. And before I realize it, there has been a holy shift. My insatiable need to prove my own goodness to God and the world fades into the background, and instead I receive truth and offer worship to the only One deserving of it.

Your Brand of Good Girl

It may sound extreme, but this has been my ugly, people-pleasing truth. If any of it resonates with you, then I would say you are a good girl too. Perhaps you grew up in the church with a good reputation and a perfect attendance at Bible school. You never experienced a period of rebellion, at least not one that is worthy to be told as a life-changing testimony. Maybe you are an optimist, someone who seems to see the

19

good in everything and everyone. You are the first to volunteer, graduated top of your class, and are constantly the dependable friend for others to lean on.

Or maybe you accepted Jesus as an adult, and though your past may be sordid, your present is predictable. Perhaps you envy the girls who seemed to get it right the first time around. You didn't grow up a good girl, and so you're doing everything you can to make up for it. At least now you are finally living life the right way—going to church, volunteering, being good—but there is still something missing that you didn't expect this side of making all the right choices.

No matter which class of good girl you find yourself in, as day fades to dusk, you begin to feel the familiar fog of anxiety, the weight and pressure of holding it together, of longing left unmet, of unexplained emptiness even in the midst of great blessing and perceived success.

For me, life was pretty well put together. I did life right. I went to church regularly. I got married and had babies in the appropriate order. I never got arrested. I recycled. I loved Jesus. But sometimes in quiet stillness, I felt an aching that wouldn't go away, a longing to *taste and see*, to live authentically free. My instinctive impulse was to find my worth in the response of the people around me, and as a result, people became measuring sticks for my goodness rather than unique expressions of God. True victory and rest were short-lived at best, and when God's truth didn't feel true, my "sometimes truth" took over.

My Sometimes Truth

- I would rather read *People* magazine than the Bible.
- I judge people who would rather read *People* magazine than the Bible.
- I am more insecure than I would ever admit.
- The weight of expectation is heavy and often unbearable.
- Comparison is a constant companion.

- I have unexplained anxiety.
- I am not the mom I thought I would be.
- I don't quite measure up.
- I cry in the shower.

When you are a believer in Jesus but you don't know what difference he makes, you are forced to depend on that which you do know. What did I know?

- I knew how to be a friend and listen with interest.
- In school, I knew how to be an A/B student.
- I knew how to get people to like me.
- I knew how to avoid conflict.
- I knew how to perform for acceptance.
- I knew how to be positive.
- I knew how to fake it when I felt negative.

And so I put all my confidence in the things that were awesome about myself and tried to hide the things that weren't. If Jesus fit in there somewhere, well then that was nice. But if he didn't, I was doing okay on my own anyway. That is, until I wasn't.

Where Are You?

Is there something you are hiding from? If you answer this question honestly, it will reveal what it is you fear. Maybe you are hiding from remembering your past, from facing regret, from what may happen in your future. Maybe you don't want to be known because you fear people might find out you are stupid or wrong or that you don't know so much after all. Maybe you are hiding from your dreams because to face them would mean admitting they are there. And to admit that they are there would mean you aren't living them after all.

something you are hiding behind? When I answer question, I discover those places where I put my trust. A hiding place is a place where we feel safe, emphasis on *feel*. I think it is a safe place to hide from the things I fear, so that is why I stay there. Maybe you hide behind your sweet personality, because to be anything other than nice would be offensive or bad or wrong. Maybe you hide behind your list of rules because you think following them is the way to be accepted by God. I hid behind all of these masks and other ones, too.

It is important to know the answers to these questions because only in identifying the lies that trigger certain reactions will we be able to receive the truth we need to replace them. For a long time, I believed I was searching for God and thought I had found him, this God who is order and control, distant and passive. I knew he so loved the world, but I didn't know his love for me. As I gazed off into the foggy distance, hoping for a glimpse of the outline of his presence, I missed the One who stood beside me, casting his shadow over me as he showered me with his love. While I thought I was searching for him, he graciously, miraculously, and intentionally found me.

There is someone you want to be, and she isn't a hiding, mask-wearing, fear-filled woman. Worry is a thief, Fear is a liar, and Anxiety is their trembling, furrow-browed baby. I have lived with this dysfunctional family for the better part of my life. Sometimes I live with them still. Worry robs me of the peace I know is available. Fear lies and says there is no peace at all. And their immature, screaming baby Anxiety keeps me up at night with her unrelenting cries of *what if?* and *what now?* and *what will they think?*

In my efforts to appease this family, I have tried hard to become the only person I believe can keep them quiet: a good person. To want to be good isn't bad. In fact, the first time we see the word "good" in the Bible is right there in Genesis: "Then God said, 'Let there be light'; and there was light. God saw that the light was good; and God separated the light from the darkness" (Gen. 1:3–4). The Hebrew word translated "good" in this creation series of verses is *towb*, meaning "good" or "beautiful."[1] God was well pleased with his creation. So much so that on the sixth day of creation, the day he created the man and woman in his image, he added another word to *towb*. The word was *meod*, meaning "diligently, muchness, force, or abundance." (Do you love that word *muchness* as much as I do?)

The Bible says this: "God saw all that He had made, and behold, it was very good." What we read as "very good," seems to mean "an abundance of beautiful" in the original Hebrew.[2] God labeled his creation diligently beautiful, or beautiful in a persistent way and in great supply. There is a place for "good" in the Bible, but it is much better than my twisted, limited, try-hard perspective of it.

I was made to be distinctly *someone*, and so were you. In the mind of God, in his vision for the world, in his idea for the universe, he made you to go in it. He had in mind a particular you. A true you. An authentic, accurate expression of himself. A woman who is more than just a watered-down version of good.

Do you know her? Or do you know only her mask? This good girl has plenty of masks to tell you about. Unlike my oversized Barbie mask, these masks feel risky to take off.

⌒ BEHIND THE MASK ⌒

Can you identify your brand of good girl? In what areas have you been tempted to depend on yourself?

What does life look like for you when you are being driven by fear? What is your "sometimes truth" that challenges Love's lead in your life?

Do you agree that the best part of hiding is being found? Why or why not?

2

....

chasing expectation

hiding behind her good performance

I wanted God, but I lived my life like I didn't need him.
—pastor's wife

*I*f the masks we wear are the false identities we show the world, then our performance is the rubber band that holds them in place. I perform so you will like me. I perform so you will think I'm okay. I perform because it's comfortable. I perform to prove my worth to you, to God, and to myself. I perform because I don't know how *not* to.

When bad girls perform to get their needs met, they get in trouble. When good girls perform to get the same thing, we get praise. That is why the hiding is so easy for us. We work hard, we do right, and we try not to ruffle feathers. And even if we do all that by the strength of our own selves, we tell ourselves it's okay. It seems to work, therefore it's acceptable. So we keep right on with life, and our masks mix with our personality and circumstance. Before we know it, we don't really know who we are, and nobody else does, either.

Expectations and Definitions

The shape and intensity of our performance comes down to two things: *expectations* and *definitions*. I have the expectation of myself to be a good girl, a good Christian, a good wife, and a good mom. Not such bad things, until you understand my own personal, twisted definition of "good." Good means I never mess up. Good means I weigh the perfect amount. Good means I can handle everything, I don't look like a fool, and I never lose my patience. Good means my husband will never be disappointed in me, my kids will always obey, and everyone basically likes me. Good means I am enough. My goodness is all about me. Not only do I want to be a good girl, a good Christian, a good wife, and a good mom, I want to be those things in front of God and everyone. I want to be good and I want you to know it.

I know in my head that my definition of good is wrong, crazy even. Still, left to my own resources, that is how I operate. If I fail to live up to my own standard of good, I label myself a failure. I lack motivation. I become indifferent. I entertain anxiety. I snap at my children. I want to be alone. I dream of Hawaiian vacations. I wallow.

But then something happens to offer a bit of encouragement, and I find the strength to redouble my efforts at goodness. I clean the house and successfully avoid the Rocky Road ice cream. Someone gives me a compliment. The weather is nice and I get a spurt of energy. I feel empowered, and so I try again. Then, I fail again. I don't like to fail and I certainly don't want you to know I've failed. And I'm embarrassed at the predictable pattern of defeat that my life has become.

So now I stand at a fork in the road: I can try to figure out a way to continue making life work on my own or I can admit defeat and accept Jesus' invitation to simply *Come*.

The first half of this book is a picture of what it looks like to choose the first way, to try to make life work on my own, to choose the way of performance. In doing so, I chase down all of those floating expectations like a woman gone mad: yours, his, hers, theirs, God's, mine, and the movies'. When I'm sure I've captured them all, I hold them in one hand with my definition of good in the other. I stir it all up thick in my proud bowl of performance, combining them so you can't tell one from another. And from the sticky mess, I craft a mask to hide the real me from the eyes of the world. I cannot possibly measure up. But I desperately want to. Good lingers just over my shoulder, taking on different roles depending on my life stage.

The Good Girl

I never seriously considered being a rebel. There was that one time in high school when I was the only one not drinking at a party. I looked around the room and briefly wondered why I felt so responsible to not be that way. I wondered why I couldn't simply lighten up and have some fun. But I just didn't have it in me. There was too much at stake. I had a good reputation to uphold, a sweetness to protect, an important list of rules to follow, and a long list of people to please.

This innate desire to be good indeed protected me from a lot of heartache and baggage. It protected me from teenage pregnancy and bad grades and jail. But it did not bring me any greater understanding of God. It did not protect me from my own impossible expectations.

Growing up a good girl was natural for me. But there were those times when it was exhausting to try to measure up. Good girls are good listeners. Good girls are always there for everyone. Good girls don't get mad. Good girls are laid-back. Good girls roll with the punches, go with the flow, follow the leader (as long as the leader is a good girl, of course).

I was a good girl and I wanted to be a good girl, but it often kept me from saying what I really meant. In fact, my desire to be good even kept me from exploring my own opinion, and I grew up to believe that my opinion didn't actually matter much anyway. I avoided vulnerability for fear of being rejected or being labeled needy. Good girls aren't needy, they are need*ed*. And so instead of living free, I lived safe.

The Good Christian

I once heard a sermon that compared believers to commercials for God. "And God doesn't need any bad commercials," I remember the preacher saying. It stuck with me, and from then on I often made decisions based on whether or not I thought it would be good advertising for God. I saw myself from the outside and thought about what type of Christian people would think me to be. Fear of rejection by other Christian peers was a powerful motivator, especially in college.

In the midnineties, I attended Bible college as an eighteen-year-old good girl. There was a group of students who would go downtown every Friday night and walk up to strangers to tell them about Jesus. I'm not sure it was the most effective way to share the Jesus story, but I suppose that is what young, energetic Bible college students do.

I hated going to street witness. It was awkward, uncomfortable, and never seemed to make any difference. Friday afternoons would find me hiding out in my dorm room to avoid the upperclassmen group gathering outside. But there was another reason I hated this Friday night activity. The reason I wasn't very motivated to share Jesus with people was because the only thing I had to tell them was "You'll go to heaven when you die." If they didn't believe in heaven, I had nothing more to say.

I didn't know any real, relevant answers to questions people were actually asking. To me, being a Christian was hard work. I secretly didn't wish that on anyone. At least those unbelievers could have fun in their ignorance. All I had was rules and guilt. Lots of guilt. I felt shame for who I was. I had to be perfect, but I wasn't. And that wasn't okay.

I worried because I thought good Christians enjoyed sharing Jesus with people. But I didn't. The way I saw life was a constant battle of trying to get something I didn't think I had, of trying to become who Jesus wanted me to be, of trying to become a better version of myself. Because this was the underlying basis for everything, the gospel didn't seem like very good news to me. I felt like I was supposed to share it, but the truth was I didn't really know what it was.

While flipping through a journal from that time in my life, I was flooded with memories of who I thought I would be by now. As a girl of only twenty, I imagined myself on the mission field translating the Bible into tribal languages and living in a land of opposition. I imagined tangible, external foes opposing me. And I imagined I would be strong enough to handle them.

Instead I became a sign language interpreter, had three kids, and live in a quiet cul-de-sac with my youth pastor husband and my stainless steel fridge. But my clamorous foes come just as readily, though perhaps not so overtly. They show up in the shape of an unlikely enemy: *my own self*. The way I hold on to expectation, the way I believe half-truths and less-than gospels, the way I forget to remember to be still.

I am struck by how I have lived in a constant state of high expectation. I compared my current life to the one I thought I would be living. I compared my Jesus walk to the way it seemed it ought to be. I had clear ideas about what important Jesus work was supposed to look like, and it had nothing to do with cleaning the toilet.

The Good Wife

He proposed on a warm night in early September. I knew it was coming, but I was shocked nonetheless. There is something about hearing a man say he wants to spend the rest of his life with you that has a way of stunning a girl's heart no matter how much she expects it. We spent the rest of that evening making phone calls to friends and family members and planning out forever over lattes and a dozen orange roses.

Though it took only nine months to plan our wedding, I had spent twenty-three years building up the expectations. They followed hard after me, seeping into every part of my days. My insatiable desire to be the perfect wife weighed heavy, but I was dangerously unaware. All of my life, I had looked forward to marriage, expecting to find over its threshold a foolproof security, an abundant assurance, and undeniable proof that I was lovely and lovable. Because all my needs would be met, I would be the best wife who ever lived.

I had heard the truth, that there was no man who could fill the ache inside from all of those empty parts that were never satisfied. I heard only Jesus could do that. Still, I thought *maybe*. Maybe our marriage will be different. Better. Other-than. Enough.

Two months after our wedding day, I found myself curled up in a ball on our still-stiff leather sofa, staring at the biggest, blankest wall in the living room of our two-bedroom condo, paralyzed with fear because I didn't know what color to paint the room. I was sobbing uncontrollably over paint.

Not only that, I hated the way I hung the pictures throughout the house. Our bedroom constantly had dirty clothes on the floor, our bathroom was in desperate need of some Clorox, and the kitchen was a disorganized mess. Of course, that shouldn't have mattered since I rarely cooked. The guest room was filled with boxes that needed emptying, a closet that needed organizing, projects that needed finishing, and a wedding gown that needed cleaning.

That's when Expectation began to speak: Good wives keep a clean house and don't cry about paint. Good wives make good food for their hungry men and anticipate their needs before they have them. And by the way? Good wives are beautiful. That gorgeous Good Wife stood in the corner of my living room, just over my husband's shoulder. She was so put-together, so strikingly perfect, and so very ashamed of me. I was a prisoner in my own home, a prisoner to my own impossible expectation.

My life was a performance that no one wanted tickets to see. Including me.

I didn't realize it at the time, but I had always believed I would become her when I got married, that perfect invisible version of myself who instinctively knew the best color to paint a wall. I realized that day on the couch that the Good Wife was a terrible friend who had stood me up in the worst way.

I wanted to wife perfectly and nest perfectly and be a woman who knew what she wanted. I felt shame at my inability to experience freedom in my home for fear of wrecking it all with my indecisiveness and my not-yet-secure taste.

As embarrassing as it is to admit, I experienced a deep sense of loss that day. All of my life, I had been able to either perform my way into success or hide successfully from my failure. But having a man right there in my living room (his living room!) watching my ridiculous breakdown, there was no hiding from him.

My expectations to be a good wife seemed so noble. The problem wasn't so much that I had expectations in myself. Instead, the problem was that my expectations were impossible, and the way I chose to live up to them was by traveling on the overused, dead-end road of performance.

The Good Mom

The life of a young mother can be a very dark place to live. People don't really talk about that at baby showers. Those early days are filled with doubt, fear, worry, and lots of epic failures. Pregnancy brought with it all kinds of crazy. I felt sick all the time and quickly began to resent the loss of appetite, energy, and perceived control. From the first twinge of guilty resentment I felt during month three of that twin pregnancy, I just knew that I would never be Good Mom, no matter how much I thought I should be.

Good Mom makes breakfast and smiles a lot. Good Mom always remembers to notice, compliment, and encourage. She is fun and funny. She plays dolls with pleasure and even makes suggestions for pretend scenarios to make the play go longer. Her patience is limitless and she never raises her voice. She wakes up early every morning and spends time with Jesus. She is consistent and kind. She makes cookies from scratch. She plays outside even when it's really hot. She builds forts with blankets in the living room. Her house is always clean, her produce is always fresh, and she has a garden with flowers and vegetables. She can sing. She makes puppets out of socks. Her kids never watch TV because they are totally satisfied to listen to the riveting, captivating stories that their Good Mom makes up. Every night.

And then there is me. I haven't worn matching socks in three years. I pulled out nine individual socks from my drawer the other day. Nine. All different. My kids fight. A lot. They call each other the biggest insult in their kindergarten-level arsenal: *baby*. And they all hate to be called babies, so of course that is their first line of defense when provoked. And it makes me crazy. I have had the same butter knife in my dishwasher for two weeks. Some unidentifiable food is stuck to one side. It's just too much to wash it by hand. And? My car has ants.

With each small discouragement, be it the messy state of my house or the messy state of my heart, I feel a little more less-than, a little further from Good Mom, a little more shamed by her. She stands in my kitchen with a ladle in her hand and her Williams-Sonoma apron on, with just enough flour on her nose to prove she's been cooking but not enough to make her look foolish. And her clean, good kids cling to those apron strings while she looks at me with pity in her eyes and shakes that ladle in my general direction, telling me what a failure I've become. I feel like there is a mom I'm supposed to be but I will never, ever measure up.

A Better Way

I could fill this book with the thousands of expectations I live under. Perhaps you could too. Expectations rule the day. My disappointment or satisfaction with a situation rests entirely upon what I expected to happen. In all these situations, what I expected to happen was up to me.

Because there is so much I believe I should be, there is also much I believe I lack. And so my tendency has been to hide.

When we believe that God expects us to try hard to become who Jesus wants us to be, we will live in that blurry, frustrating land of Should Be rather than trust in The One Who Is. We will do whatever we believe it takes to please God rather than receive the acceptance that has already been given. We will perform to live up to what we believe his expectation is of us rather than expectantly wait on him.

Expectations aren't inherently bad things. But I think they are misused by good girls. Jesus didn't put expectations on himself. He didn't micromanage his own image and constantly try to align his reality with his ideal. Instead, he lived expectantly, waiting for the next step. His was a life of total and complete dependence and submission to the voice and will of his Father. In the Psalms, David seemed to understand this as well: "My soul, wait only upon God and silently submit to Him; for my hope and expectation are from Him" (Ps. 62:5 AMP).

Our desire to be the good girl, the good Christian, the good wife, and the good mom becomes our number one priority, and Jesus isn't even in the room. Our failures expose us and so we hide them. We hide us. We work hard to perform for acceptance, and most of the time we don't even realize we are doing it. It has become the natural way of things, the only way we know to live. Perhaps it is the way our moms did it and their moms before them. It is the way of survival. This heavy weight of expectation is not easily lifted, because most of the time the good girls' compulsion to live up to impossible expectations stems from beliefs that are formed in early childhood and manifest themselves throughout our lives. No one knows that better than Lucy.

Lucy's Story

When I first met Lucy, I subconsciously labeled her as just like me only better. We had a lot in common. We both loved *Real Simple* magazine, we both worked with the youth group, and we even liked the same TV shows. But she seemed more put together than I was. She didn't just read *Real Simple*, she cut out articles and organized them into an intricate filing system according to topic. She was such a good girl. She didn't just clean her house, she had a schedule posted on her fridge of which tasks to do each day. She was such a good wife. She led a small group and went on every youth trip and seemed to be the leader all the girls looked up to and wanted to be just like. She was such a good Christian. I liked her immediately and wanted to know her better. But there was something about her that kept me at arm's length. After hearing her story, I now know what it was. Lucy was in hiding.

On the outside, Lucy's childhood home looked like every other. But when she was eight and her mom announced she would be having another baby, Lucy's world began to shift. Her father was not happy about the pregnancy. He was angry and said he wished it weren't true. As an eight-year-old, Lucy wondered if her father had felt the same way when she was born.

She began to form an image of herself that day. She began to see herself as unwanted. The sin of her father opened wide the door to an unwelcome guest: the lie. The first lie she believed: *I am worthless.*

As an adult looking back, she realized that her father was a narcissist. He was selfish and self-centered and was unable or unwilling to take care of anyone but himself. Lucy felt rejected by her father, which led to a false belief that she was worthless and unwanted. But she didn't want anyone to know that she was worthless and unwanted, so she set out to prove her own worth by becoming the best at everything.

She did a fantastic job.

Enter lie number two: *I have worth because I perform well.*

Her mom got sick when she was ten, so she and her little brother were left in the care of their father, a father who was unfit for the job. Lucy took care of herself. She made spaghetti, swept floors, and made sure her baby brother was okay. She remembers hearing *Sesame Street* playing in the living room but not having time to sit and watch. There was too much work to do.

Can you even imagine a ten-year-old carrying the weight of her world on her own tiny shoulders? Things were not as they should be. Little girls are to be protected. They should not have to protect themselves.

During this time Lucy began to believe that she could not trust anyone but herself. No one would take care of her. Rather than collapse in despair or self-pity, she chose instead to craft a mask of strength and responsibility. *I can handle this*, she told herself. And she did.

That solidified lie number three: *The only person I can ever depend on is me.*

She excelled in school and the arts and rose to the top of whatever club or group she joined. All of her success began to communicate one overarching belief: *I am better than everyone, because look at what I've survived.* She had figured out how to make life work without anyone else. The only problem in the midst of all that success was that she was not free. Behind her masks of strength, responsibility, and good performance, she was a tangled mess. And she was all alone.

No one really knew Lucy because Lucy didn't really know herself. The sweet good news of Jesus is that he longs to call us out from behind those masks we wear to hide our mess from the world. Lucy was no exception.

We were all grown up and married and she had success-fully kept all of her friends at a long arm's length. While on a trip together, one of her longtime friends told Lucy that she felt she didn't really know her: "You know everything about me, my struggles, my issues, and my junk. I've known you forever, but I don't know you at all."

In the spirit of wanting to be a good friend, Lucy began to tell her story. She was guarded at first, but there came a point when she realized she was holding back. That was when the floodgates opened. Out it spilled: the selfishness of her father, the abuse the family experienced at his hand, the heartache of her mom's sickness, and the responsibility she felt for all of it. Once the tears began, they didn't stop. As she talked, it was as if those masks were melting off before our eyes. When she was finished, she sat there feeling empty, wondering who she was without them. She went home broken and exposed.

In her desperate, needy state, she began to read Psalm 63, and this is what it said: "For You have been my help, and in the shadow of Your wings I sing for joy" (Ps. 63:7). In that moment, it was as if the truth winked brightly up at her from the pages of her Bible. Because she was no longer reading through the filter of her masks, Lucy realized in those words that she didn't have to hide anymore. She didn't have to perform to prove her worth. She didn't have to take care of herself. Though there would be months of healing ahead for her, the firstfruits of freedom began to bloom in her that day.

In their book *TrueFaced*, Bill Thrall, Bruce McNicol, and John Lynch powerfully identify the root of the mask: "Mask-wearing, though a horrible problem, is not the underlying problem. It is the pitiful symptom of the larger problem: unresolved sin issues. A mask is only the public proof that an infection is spreading through my body. Inside me, there is a seditious, self-destructive process compelling me to hide what is really true about me."[1]

Lucy's story is a great example of how the unresolved sin of her father manifested itself in her own life. Her hurt response was an indication that healing and wholeness was needed. But Lucy was just a kid, so she did the only thing she knew: she fashioned a mask and hid behind it. It was the only way she knew to stay safe from more hurt.

As good girls, we subconsciously label ourselves as the strong ones, the responsible ones, the sweet ones, or the right ones. We try to stand tall and capable as the good Christian, the good wife, the good mom, and the good one. But Jesus is calling us to a deeper, truer, freer identity. All he wants is simply you—minus your good works, minus your perfect attendance, minus your politeness. When you really believe that, you may discover that all you want is Jesus, simply Jesus. Not just to get to heaven or to help you be a good person or do the right thing, but to simply love and be loved by him.

⧫ BEHIND THE MASK ⧫

The way I defined being good in my life was overblown and exaggerated. Do you have a definition of good that may be twisted or irrational? What is it?

Describe your invisible good girl, good Christian, good wife, or good mom. What does she look like? Who does she sound like? How do you feel sitting next to her?

What aspects of your performance are you unwilling to let go? What do you think will happen if you do?

What does living safely look like for you? How would things be different if you could live free?

Read Psalm 139:14: "I will give thanks to You, for I am fearfully and wonderfully made; wonderful are Your works, and my soul knows it very well." The thoughts we practice tend to become the truths we live. What thoughts do you tend to dwell on as a good girl? What does your soul know very well? Fear? Anxiety? Worry? Discontentment? What would it take for your soul to know love and acceptance?

3

....

my not-so-extreme makeover

hiding behind her good reputation

Not that we are adequate in ourselves to consider anything
as coming from ourselves, but our adequacy is from God.

—2 Corinthians 3:5

Extreme Makeover: Home Edition was one of my favorite shows for a while, mainly because I loved to see the before and after shots. The water damage in the bathroom, the rotting ceiling beams, and the messy kids' rooms were all so extremely awful. Then *poof!* They move that bus and before our eyes is a new, beautiful, complete house. No more rot, no more mold; a clean, fresh house with flat-screen TVs and themed bedrooms for the kids.

Makeover shows are compelling for one reason: we love to see the bad turn good. To watch something that was falling apart be restored and renewed is encouraging and hopeful. It's the same way with people.

Growing up in the church, I heard a lot of testimonies from people who went from bad to Jesus. Their lives consisted of one bad decision after another, which is what made their story so powerful. From alcohol, drugs, sex, and cigarettes, their rebellion would lead to a dramatic climax. Jesus showed up and their lives looked completely different. There was no denying that God got the credit.

As a girl who accepted Jesus at a young age, I couldn't relate. In fact, I admit to sometimes wishing I had a few years of rebellion under my belt. Then my story would be interesting and dramatic too.

Small-Town Girl

Growing up in a small, southern Indiana town, my sister and I didn't have a whole lot of ways to get into trouble. We spent our summer days playing outside until it got dark and the lightning bugs came out. We played Barbies and waited for pregnant cats to give birth to litters of kittens. We had lemonade stands and drank most of it before earning any money. We practiced the moonwalk but always did it opposite and couldn't figure out why our Ked-covered feet didn't look like Michael Jackson's. We did normal 1980s kid things.

Our very loving and slightly overprotective mother had clear rules about things we were and were not allowed to do. We were allowed to walk down the back alley to Melissa's house as long as we stayed together. We were allowed to walk the half block to the convenience store for a Coke and a cherry Blow Pop as long as Mom was watching from the front porch. We were also allowed to ride bikes on the road as long as we stayed on the gravel side.

We were not, under any circumstances, allowed to go under the bridge. Apparently, that was where all kinds of awful happened. I never knew exactly what was so bad about the bridge, but in the depths of my imagination I saw hordes of witches crouched in the dark, stirring their steaming brew, buying the souls of unsuspecting seven-year-olds in cutoff shorts sporting skinned-up knees. To go under the bridge was the ultimate declaration of independence from adult wisdom or supervision. To go under the bridge was to be a rebel.

Nearly four years older, my sister and her friends determined how the days would be filled. I got to tag along because I complained and Mom felt sorry for me. I don't remember anything about what happened under the bridge the day we broke the rule. All I remember is how I felt afterward. Guilty. I believed my role in the family was to be the good girl, the one who never got into trouble, the one with the admirable reputation. I had an overwhelming compulsion to confess to my mother. I remember sitting next to her, knowing I couldn't carry the burden of my disobedience any longer, despite the earlier pleas from my big sister to keep my mouth shut. I'm sure we were punished for doing something we weren't supposed to, and I'm also sure that I was punished less than my older sister. I probably cried. I was the baby, after all.

My reaction to disobedience was just as it should have been: guilt. But it didn't come about as a conviction of the Holy Spirit or a sense that I had sinned. I was simply a good girl with a heavy, innate sense of right and wrong and an extra dose of responsibility.

The Life of a Good Girl

Even after I prayed to receive Jesus and was baptized at the front of that small church in the middle of a cornfield, it was that inner sense of responsibility that continued to influence the way I lived and the choices I made. Even though I was a believer, it didn't make much difference in the way I lived. I was good before Jesus. I was good after Jesus. No fireworks. No parades. No dramatic turnarounds.

And so it was that I continued with my good way of life, giving myself credit for all of my own goodness. There was a sense that Jesus had something to do with it, as I clearly remember sitting on the playground under the monkey bars in the first grade telling my best friend all about how Jesus died for her and doesn't she want to accept him too? But I didn't understand the middle-of-a-Tuesday Jesus. I only knew him as a when-I-get-to-heaven Jesus. Salvation was my ticket to heaven and not much else.

At thirteen I rededicated my life to the Lord because I was scared to death that perhaps it didn't take the first time. I stared at my feet as I walked up that orange-carpeted aisle and stood next to the pastor while all the grown-ups filed by with pleased looks and proud words. All I could think was, *I can't wait to get out of here and what's for lunch, anyway?*

As I got older and entered high school, my story never included anything scandalous. I didn't have sex with boys for two reasons: I was scared of them, and they didn't ask me to, anyway. I was good because I was afraid of boys, afraid of hell, and afraid of getting into trouble. I knew how to listen to the spirit of fear. I had not yet learned the voice of the Spirit of God.

The Mask Wearing Begins

Author David Seamands once wrote, "Children are the best recorders but the worst interpreters."[1] I remember a lot about being a kid. I remember colors and moments, arguments and smells, situations and conversations that are just as vivid as if I lived them yesterday. Though my memories may be clear, I extract meaning from those memories that may or may not be.

So that big kid who sat three rows in front of me on the bleachers in the fifth grade and turned around and called me Dumbo because my ears stuck out? That memory is vivid in my mind. I can hear the squeaks of the players' shoes in the background, smell the rubber mixed with sweat and floor wax, and see those boys in front of me with their hooded sweatshirts and their sneering grins: *great recorder.* But the sinking feeling I had after that night and the voice that spoke in my head for years after that, causing me to avoid ponytails and always have my hair down: *bad interpreter*. My kid brain wasn't capable of reason, so the memory stuck and served to shape my actions and beliefs as I grew up. And even though I'm a grown-up now and I can rationalize that those boys were simply insecure and thoughtless, it doesn't change my mind. I still believe what they said even though I am grown.

It works in positive ways, too. I was praised a lot as a kid. My parents' friends and extended family members commented on what a good girl I was, teachers boasted about my behavior in school, and I rarely got in trouble at home. I put a lot of confidence in myself and in my good reputation.

I was a good recorder of the praise and the accolades from the grown-ups who thought I was strong and capable. I remember their words and proud looks. I treasured their admiration of me. But instead of simply interpreting their words as encouragement, I internalized them and let them become a standard to continue reaching for. I put extreme pressure on myself to live up to the good girl in their minds. I wanted people to see me as able, even as young as elementary school. I let their proud words define me and lead me to a puffed-up self-dependence, leaving little room for Jesus.

That's how the mask wearing begins. The neglect of Lucy's father led her to believe things about herself that weren't true. For everyone, something happens that leads to a feeling, be it rejection or fear or elation or pride. And that feeling becomes a belief deeply ingrained and carefully coddled. In turn, that belief turns into ways we choose to cope with things and live our lives.

So my good reputation was where I began to place my identity. Though my good started out motivated by fear, it slowly started to pay off. I was the girl who did things right; the friend others came to when they needed advice; the girl on the outskirts of drama; the sensible, cheerful friend. My goodness became part of my identity. Soon, boys liked me *because of* my good reputation. The right kind of boys.

Good Girl Meets Good Boy

Tenth grade was the year I got my braces off, earned my driver's license, and befriended a guy one year ahead of me. He had majorly high moral standards. He was athletic and well liked. He didn't party like those around him, but he still managed to fit in with them. They respected him for his moral right-ness. Just like they respected me. He was my first real boyfriend.

I didn't realize it at the time, but I was a good girl desperate for male attention. It could have been because I grew up in a home with an alcoholic father, or it could have just been because I was human. Whatever the reason, I was a well-adjusted, confident, healthy girl on the outside who was desperate for male attention, affirmation, and love on the inside. Even though we were very young, I had my first glimpse of what it might feel like to be loved in a romantic way. It didn't take long for me to become addicted to that feeling.

We were created with a deep need for love, acceptance, worth, and security. The need is overwhelming and must be satisfied. In the same way some girls wear the mask of promiscuity to grasp for connection and acceptance, good girls can depend on their good reputation to meet their desperate need for love. Even though it looked good and healthy on the outside, this relationship was a significant source of acceptance for me and began an unhealthy pattern of looking to men to affirm my identity.

Good Girl Grows Up

My reputation isn't only defined by what I did or did not do with boys. Reputation can be built in lots of ways. The apostle Paul describes his reputation in great detail in Philippians 3:1–11. Consider the credentials Paul lists there: circumcised on the eighth day, of the nation of Israel, of the tribe of Benjamin, a Hebrew of Hebrews, a zealous persecutor of the church, righteous and blameless in his keeping of the Law. He had an impeccable reputation in nearly every area of life—religious, genetic, and political. And that was all before he met Jesus.

Many good girls can relate with Paul's impeccable reputation. We are the daughters of pastors and missionaries, we support the "right" candidates in the polls, we attended Bible college. We homeschool our children or we send them to private Christian schools or we are the presidents of the public school PTA. We marry pastors, we lead Bible studies, we sing in the choir, we volunteer in the nursery. And sometimes we do those things in response to Jesus' leading. But sometimes, we do them to maintain our good reputation.

I am not typically the first person to volunteer for things. But when I do, you can certainly depend on me. It is good and right and responsible to follow through in those things we have committed to. I would never deny that. But there are times when I have become involved in a committee or volunteered for a position that seems to run its course and I sense the Holy Spirit leading me away from that thing or that place of service. But instead of prayerfully considering a change, I struggle and fight against it for fear of what others might think of my backing down.

As a good girl, it is hard to risk quitting commitments for fear of how it might look to those watching. Rather than listening to God's gentle leading in those areas, I fear and I fret that my reputation as *the dependable one* or as *the one who can handle things* will be threatened.

The Mess behind the Mask

The mask of the good reputation is a hard one to take off. So much of who I am is wrapped up in what I do or in what I have abstained from all my life. While it is true that Jesus calls us to live a holy, set-apart life, he doesn't do so in order for us to gain something from him. And his idea of holy and set apart may be shockingly different from what we always thought.

A girl with a good reputation easily makes friends at Bible college, effortlessly impresses the parents of boyfriends, and has little trouble coasting into the role of pastor's wife. But if she hides behind her good reputation, there is little room for correction, and the good girl is in danger of being her own compass rather than having a softened heart to the leading of God as he speaks through his Word, friends, or family members. There could be a fear of intimacy, because people who get too close might see things she wishes weren't there. Hiding behind that good-looking mask, her arms are folded too tightly to give and receive grace, or to fall into an embrace from a God who sees beyond her good reputation.

Behavior matters. Decisions matter. Sin has consequences. In fact, sin is too serious an issue for God to leave it up to us to fix or make right on our own (we'll explore this more in Chapter 10). It would be years before I would understand the dangers of this moral obsession with my right-ness or wrong-ness being based on my performance. I subconsciously categorized people into classes of either right or rebellious rather than seeing them as people in desperate need of God.

As a good girl, I formed my own definition of sin rather than understand God's. Sin was the bad stuff people do, the heartache people cause, the poor decisions people make. But my insatiable desire to be my own little god somehow didn't make the list of sin in my book. My incessant need to be better than, to be important, to be liked and right and good on my own and by myself—those things pulsed just under the surface of my smiling exterior.

In Christian circles, we tend to call that self-righteousness. And it is. We could also call it self-dependence, and this gospel of self-sufficiency robs good girls of a life of freedom and victory.

My Present-Day Reputation

While my reputation in high school depended heavily upon what I did (or more specifically, *did not do*) with boys, the mask of the good reputation still shows up in my adult life. But it looks different now.

While preparing the manuscript for this book, I wanted to interview a few writers of blogs that I read, as I was convinced their stories would resonate with good girls everywhere. One blogger in particular was my friend Kelly.

I have never met Kelly in real life, though I am an avid reader of her blog. She agreed to chat with me on the phone. One afternoon I called her up at the time we had agreed upon, and I spent about thirty minutes asking her questions and listening to her story. A few weeks later, I received this email from Kelly:

> I've been meaning to email you since our phone conversation. I didn't think calling would be weird at all until you were on the phone and for some inexplicable reason I started shaking and babbling. I had to sit down to talk to you, because I started getting chills. I was so embarrassed over what I said or didn't say that I went into hiding for a while. I have needed to write to you, to thank you for calling me, to tell you that I loved your voice and your accent, and to tell you I am sorry I was so nervous. I'm not a groupie type of person. My reaction surprised me so much.
>
> I wanted to tell you this, because you're not just a blog friend after a phone call. I encountered you in person and your person was sweet and wonderful and cool and my person was not so cool and felt so inadequate to have a conversation with you. I said things I might not have written or that would have come out better in writing than in my half-panicked person voice.

I wrote her back and assured her not to feel embarrassed, that she was charming and helpful and fantastic. But what I didn't tell her was this: *I was a wreck before I called her.* I was nervous and sweaty and I didn't want to do it. As 2:00 p.m. grew closer, I tried to figure a way to get out of it, but I knew I couldn't. The call was my idea! The thing about blogging is you get to put your best foot forward. You get to edit and delete and ponder before you actually say anything. You get to manage your own reputation. I was worried that when she finally heard me speak unedited, she would see me for who I really am, and then she wouldn't like me anymore.

Kelly's email response showed me she was feeling the same way! But instead of writing honestly back to her and admitting my own insecurities, I straightened up my mask of that good reputation without even realizing I was doing it. I took her email as confirmation that my reputation was still intact: *Good. She thinks I'm cool and awesome. No need to tell her I was a hot mess before we spoke. I'll just let her be the mess.* What a mess, indeed.

The Reputation of Jesus

Character refers to who you are. Reputation refers to who people think you are. I generally care more about who people think I am than who I really am. But Jesus was not a person trying to keep a good reputation intact. During his life on earth, he never tried to explain himself for the sake of his reputation.

In his book *Breaking the Rules*, Fil Anderson talks about the scandalous reputation of Jesus:

> He breaks all social etiquette in relating to people. He acknowledges no barriers or human divisions. There is no category of sinners he isolates himself from. Simply stated, Jesus is a miserable failure at meeting religious people's expectations of him. He connects with the kinds of people he should disregard. He attends the wrong dinner parties. He is rude to respected religious leaders and polite to whores. He reprimands his own followers and praises outsiders and riffraff.[2]

He healed people, but he didn't heal everyone. He stirred things up wherever he went, and the Pharisees hated the fact

47

that he existed. He associated with adulterous and unclean women, lepers, and tax collectors. Though he was without sin, there were still those who questioned his reputation. Knowing there were people who disagreed, even hated him, didn't cause him to change one thing he did. He wasn't working to maintain a good reputation. He was walking in dependence on his Father. Jesus didn't value what people thought; he valued people, period.

By refusing to level with Kelly and take off my mask to reveal our common frailty, I kept her at arm's length. I may have kept my cool reputation intact, but I did not offer her any human connection. In that moment, I chose my reputation over authentic relationship. That is not the way I want to live. What about you?

ᖇᖇ Behind the Mask ᖇᖇ

Walk back through your history to a point in time, maybe within the first ten years of your life, where you recall a memory that may have encouraged you to begin maintaining your reputation. What was the circumstance?

If you were a good girl before Jesus and you're still good now, then what changed? What happened for you at salvation? What were you saved from?

What have you been doing to satisfy your needs for belonging, worth, and love?

What would be a reputation nightmare for you? Name it. Describe it.

Read Philippians 3:1–11 again. What words does Paul use to describe his reputation in comparison with knowing Jesus?

4

....

with a wink and a smile

hiding behind her fake "fine"

I've been carefully tucking away my heart, because I am terrified that if anyone saw it as it really is, they would run in the other direction.

—Kristen, a recovering good girl

Even in laughter the heart may ache, and joy may end in grief.

—Proverbs 14:13 NIV

*I*t was raining the day Helen was buried. I didn't know her personally, but she was the mother of a dear friend. Helen had been battling cancer for some time before she died. Her life had not been easy. During the funeral, I sat in the back and listened to the people who knew her well talk about her life and legacy. It was lovely.

The pastor spoke of her with fondness and admiration. "She never complained," he said, "she never let on that she was suffering." These words of praise from a man of faith left me wondering what people would say about me at my funeral. Would I be able to suffer with cancer and never let on I was suffering? Would I even *want* to never let on I was suffering?

We praise people who never let on they are suffering.

One afternoon in my car, I listened as a man called in to a radio show. He had been a soldier stationed in Iraq. Upon returning to the States, a deep depression settled over him from which there was no escape. But he didn't seek help. Years before, this same man walked around with a broken foot for two years before he sought medical attention. He was so accustomed to functioning in a culture of strength that he believed to seek advice for a mental ailment would be a threat to his career.

We praise people who remain strong, no matter their pain.

Sara has dealt with depression her whole life but hides it well.

> I can put a smile on my face no matter what. Most people don't even know I deal with depression; most don't know how severely it affects my life. When I have called in sick at work, I can't let myself even sound sick. When I talk to someone on the phone I put on the mask and sound perfectly fine no matter how ill I am. Now my mother is deathly ill and I feel like I have put on a new mask. People ask how she is doing but I don't know if they are really interested. I fight these masks but I can't seem to remove them. I want someone to care, I want someone to call me and ask how I am, but what will be my answer, I'm not sure. I feel like I'm whining if I tell the truth, but I need someone to be my support.[1]

The Fearful Fine

A dying woman won't let on that she suffers. A depressed soldier fears for his job. A daughter hides behind a pleasant mask because she doesn't want to sound whiny. All of these people had very serious reasons why they hid behind a fake "fine." I tell their stories to illustrate how "fining" our way through life can lead down a very dark, lonely road. Clearly, I'm no medical professional and am in no way attempting to give bubblegum answers to serious issues. However, many good girls have a natural disposition of sweetness that can morph into a mask of false happiness and steal authentic joy that comes from the Lord. We value harmony above our own opinions or emotions, and we smile and smooth over rather than risk disappointment or worse, rejection.

Not all good girls hide behind their fake fines, but for those of us who do, this mask might be the most suffocating of all. We insult the beauty of intimacy and sometimes even risk our own health for the sake of keeping everything fine.

My friend Holley and her husband tried for years to become pregnant only to be met, time and time again, with negative pregnancy tests. "I'd been one of those people who always said, 'I'm fine' when anyone asked. But I got to a place where that was no longer an option. I remember worrying what people would think or how God would feel. One of the things that kept me from admitting I wasn't okay is that I thought I had to be perfect or whole to be used by God."[2] Holley is still waiting for a baby, but she is no longer doing so behind a mask of fine. She sits in the midst of a hard-won peace, the kind she says comes after war.[3] But so often, the idea that we have to keep it together no matter what is what keeps good girls from coming out from behind our sweet, smiling exteriors. We believe that any amount of broken mess disqualifies us from useful activity for God, so we determine to stay decidedly unbroken.

Tammy Maltby believed that, too. In her book, *Confessions of a Good Christian Girl*, Tammy explains what was happening on the inside during the darkest, most difficult time of her life.

Emotionally and relationally, my world was falling apart, and I was holding on for dear life to keep it from collapsing entirely and leaving me out in the cold. But nothing I tried seemed to work. I dredged up endless Bible verses. They all sounded empty in my ears. I prayed desperately for relief. It didn't come. I read countless self-help books. Their pat answers and quick fixes just annoyed me. I cried, fasted, begged God to rescue me. The chasm just widened, and the winter wind howled even louder. . . . When I finally let go of my sunny, successful façade . . . when I finally dared to acknowledge the cold in my heart . . . when my false reality shattered and I finally reached the end of myself . . . God was there. At the bottom of my personal pit—that's where I rediscovered His outlandish, outrageous, incredible gift.[4]

Though these were the darkest days of her life, Tammy admits they were a necessary turning point for her. In order for her to receive the gift of God's unconditional love and acceptance for her, she had to come to a place of surrender and brokenness. She had to give up fine.

To Be Julia

When I was in the fourth grade, my family moved six hours away from my Indiana hometown. I started out as the shy girl and kept to myself. But in our new home in Iowa during the summer of 1988, shy got me nowhere. I quickly made friends with Jessica across the street and Sarah on the corner by being fun and happy. Accommodating. Pleasant. Able to blend. I was a human chameleon, and I didn't even know it. I continued with that way of coping for many years. I didn't realize it was coping; I just thought it was me. *I'm laid-back. Things don't bother me. I'm easy to get along with.*

And I was, until I got hurt. And when I got hurt, rather than facing the hurt and being honest about the fact that it was there, I hid the hurt behind my mask and hoped it would fade away. Instead, it seeped into my skin and came out in other ugly ways: passivity, disconnectedness, anger. I didn't know how to share the hurt. And so it festered, I hid, and the mask got tighter.

Around that time, the show *Designing Women* was on the air. In it, sisters Julia and Suzanne Sugarbaker were as opposite as opposite gets. Julia was a sophisticated intellect and Suzanne was a showy former beauty queen. Together they ran an interior design firm out of their home. As a good girl who didn't like to ruffle feathers, I was always especially impressed with Julia Sugarbaker's ability to speak her mind without fear of what others thought of her. Here is a portion of a scene in one of the show's earliest episodes.

[After Suzanne overhears a cruel comment about her, Julia defends her sister.]

Julia: Excuse me, aren't you Marjorie Leigh Winnick, the current Miss Georgia World?

Marjorie: Why, yes I am.

Julia: I'm Julia Sugarbaker, Suzanne Sugarbaker's sister. I couldn't help overhearing part of your conversation.

Marjorie: Well, I'm sorry. I didn't know anyone was here.

Julia: Yes, and I gather from your comments there are a couple of other things you don't know, Marjorie. For example, you probably didn't know that Suzanne was the only contestant in Georgia pageant history to sweep every category except congeniality, and that is not something the women in my family aspire to anyway. Or that when she walked down the runway in her swimsuit, five contestants quit on the spot. Or that when she emerged from the isolation booth to answer the question, "What would you do to prevent war?" she spoke so eloquently of patriotism, battlefields, and diamond tiaras, grown men wept. And you probably didn't know, Marjorie, that Suzanne was not just any Miss Georgia, she was THE Miss Georgia. She didn't twirl just a baton, that baton was on fire. And when she threw that baton into the air, it flew higher, further, faster than any baton has ever flown before, hitting a transformer and showering the darkened arena with sparks! And when it finally did come down, Marjorie, my sister caught that baton, and twelve thousand people jumped to their feet for sixteen and one-half minutes of uninterrupted thunderous ovation, as flames illuminated her tear-stained face! And that, Marjorie—just so you will know—and your children will someday know—is the night the lights went out in Georgia![5]

Isn't that fantastic? Don't you want to stand up and clap along with those twelve thousand people!? Oh, how I wish I could pull out my inner Julia Sugarbaker a time or two. It would feel so amazingly liberating to just tell it like it is. I can't tell you how many times I have stood dumbfounded and wimpy in the middle of a heated discussion only to tell the person off while alone in my car on the way home. I sound so tough alone in my car.

But is there an option besides passive compliance and Julia's tirades? Is there a way to be honestly, blamelessly emotional? Is there a way to take off the mask of the fake fine, to speak the truth and not sin?

In order to discover that option, I have to confront what I believe about my moods. As a good girl, I tend to think in extremes. Just as decisions are either right or wrong, emotions are either good or bad.

Happy? Good.
Sad? Bad.

Joyful? Good.

Disappointed? Bad.

Compliant? Good.

Confrontational? Bad.

There is no place in the Bible where it says emotions are categorized as right or wrong. Still, for a good girl in hiding, it feels risky to be honest about them. Honest could ruffle feathers. Honest could reveal differing opinions. Honest could disrupt your perception of me. Honest could ruin my carefully crafted laid-back image.

Feeling scared meant I needed more faith. Feeling anger meant I needed more control. Feeling confused meant I needed to get it together and figure things out. In theory, I knew I was supposed to cast my fear, anger, and confusion on the Lord. But after "trusting" him with my circumstances, I thought it was my responsibility to change the emotions and keep myself from experiencing them again.

The Lazy Fine

Hiding behind fine isn't always an indicator of fear. Sometimes it just takes too much energy to be authentic. I want to turn my emotions off, put my hurt up on the shelf, set the glaze in my eyes and the half-smile on my face. Not necessarily because it feels safer, but because I am lazy. And just like people who struggle with emotional eating or excessive exercise or any other type of addiction, I recognize my addiction to wanting to be left alone. I am addicted to the island of myself. The longer I hide behind fine, the easier it is to convince myself I *am* fine. I can coast that way for a while, until I start to get cranky and irritable and cross.

Mousey acceptance of my situation and hurt is not the road to freedom. Neither is Julia Sugarbakering my way through life or staying quiet because it's easier. Honesty before God is the only safe place, and I believe he is wise enough and loving enough and intuitive enough to usher us into honesty with people. Only in his presence will I be able to confront someone who has wronged me, trust someone with my messy emotions, or forgive someone in my heart. Only as I depend on and trust in and fully disclose to the One who knows anyway will I be able to discern when I'm fine-ing someone who deserves genuine. We don't have to tell everyone how we are doing. In fact, that would be a problem all by itself, trying to be intimate and vulnerable with everyone. But it is important that we tell *someone*. A lot of my own heartache and struggles with the fake fine mask could be overcome if I simply allowed myself to be honest with God and trust him to lead me in being vulnerable with people.

In the Psalms, David says things to God I wouldn't dare think on my worst days. In his anger and fear, he talks about horrible things happening to his enemies and the children of his enemies. I'm not saying those verses are instructional; I am saying that they are informative. David was nothing if not honest before God.

Turn, Turn, Turn

David's son, Solomon, could have had anything he asked from God. He chose to ask for wisdom, and so he was granted more wisdom than any man, ever. In the book of Ecclesiastes, we read his observations on how these earthly things go.

In the third chapter, he says there is a time for everything. For war as well as peace. For love as well as hate. For living as well as dying.

I saw this chapter printed out and posted to a bulletin board in the hallway of my son's preschool. "There is an appointed time for everything. And there is a time for every event under heaven." I continued to read and realized the middle of verse 8 was left out, so it simply said "a time to love and a time for peace," taking out the war and hate part. The truth is, I like their version better too. Isn't that just like a good girl? Let's overlook the hate and war parts and just be loving and peaceful. Good girls don't like that our Bible says there is a time to hate and a time for war. So we take it out.

I can't read these verses without silently inserting "turn, turn, turn" (can you?), but that is the truth of it. There is a natural rhythm to life, an ebb and flow that we can't bypass or ignore. There is no override button. Time turns and turns and rolls over itself, the awful and the lovely mixing in like colored Play-Doh. I can't say that the awful makes the lovely more lovely, because I think the lovely would be just fine all by itself. Somehow, though, it can be redeemed—even the hate and the war parts. As much as I'd prefer only the lovely, beauty from ashes tells a more compelling story.

Hiding behind fine in the midst of God and everyone is insulting to the cosmic swing God set into motion. So often I feel embarrassed or guilty over my humanness, but our emotions and experiences are all a part of that swing. They add color and dimension and life. We try to hide them behind one-dimensional masks because we believe they indicate weakness or we consider them to simply be too much trouble to dissect. Trying not to experience the whole spectrum of emotions is like trying to be inhuman. It can be especially frustrating when our emotions are the result of thinking and feeling things we know are contrary to God's truth. It doesn't seem okay to swing back and forth between believing truth and believing lies.

In their book, *The Rest of the Gospel*, Dan Stone and Greg Smith talk about this swing. "Our soul fluctuates between thoughts and feelings we don't like and thoughts and feelings we do like, and we don't like those fluctuations . . . we try to stop that swing, because our soul's fluctuations are unpleasant to us and it seems as if God wants us to stop them. We think that Christian maturity is getting that swing under control."[6]

They go on to explain why God put this swing into motion in the first place: "God designed us on the soul level to be capable of feeling and thinking things that are contrary to spirit reality. Why? Because that is the only way we can learn to live by faith out of who we really are and who He really is, rather than out of appearances."[7]

Our fluctuating humanness is there on purpose, to remind us of our need and draw us to the One who can meet it. We don't have to figure out the whys and the origins of every swinging emotion. But it is so important that we admit they are there. To embrace the color and fullness of our emotional, un-fine state is to open wide enough to receive compassion and grace. Only then will we be able to offer that same compassion and grace to others in honest and authentic ways.

Behind the Mask

Is "fine" your default? If so, do you think it is because you are afraid, lazy, or something else?

Are you in the habit of categorizing your emotions into good and bad columns? In your experience, which emotions are acceptable and which ones are unacceptable?

Can you think of any situation where it is either unacceptable or inappropriate to give an answer *other* than "fine"?

5

....

martha and my many things

hiding behind her acts of service

This is a Savior who accepts us just the way we are—Mary
or Martha or a combination of both—but loves us too much
to leave us that way. He is the one who can give us a Mary
heart in a Martha world.

—Joanna Weaver, *Having a Mary Heart in a Martha World*

My husband is the youth pastor to a large group of high school students. Every summer, he (along with about thirty other adult volunteers) takes two hundred of these students on a service mission trip called Project Serve. They spend their week painting houses, cleaning parks, hosting VBS for kids, and doing all sorts of other service-type things. Last summer was the twenty-fourth Project Serve. It is the most anticipated and well-attended trip our youth group takes.

I have not yet attended one of these trips because our kids are still young. I will never forget the time my husband, John, returned home from his first Project Serve. I was hit with some powerful and unexpected emotions of insignificance. Though I was proud of and thankful for him, I felt so very insignificant in his shadow. I felt small, hidden, overlooked, and guilty.

What kind of pastor's wife cries after her husband comes home from a mission trip? I should be happy, thankful, and free. Instead I felt lost in the shadow of his grand service trip. It seemed to me that I was expected to be supportive and refreshed, happy to welcome him home and allow him to rest after his hardworking trip. In reality, I needed a vacation from being with the kids for nine days without him.

But I felt guilty for feeling this way. More deeply though, it seemed I believed that the work he was doing as a youth pastor was somehow superior to the work I was doing at home. Anyone can be a mom. What I do is expected. What he does is extraordinary.

And there it was in all of its ugly truth. I had heard the Mother's Day sermons that praise moms for the work we do. I knew the one-liners about *changing the world one diaper at a time* and all that. I believed those things to be true. But when you are in it, it doesn't feel true. It just feels ordinary.

Maybe you aren't a mom, but you feel this way at your office or in school as you work toward your degree. Maybe you even work in a church but feel as though your job isn't one of the important ones. Maybe you can relate to feeling vanilla-grey, like your work is ordinary, or what you do is somehow not enough. Maybe you are haunted with whispers that challenge and threaten: *The work you do isn't very important. You are ordinary, less-than, and unnoticed.*

In the midst of my insecure emotions, I picked up a book written by Major Ian Thomas called *The Indwelling Life of Christ*. My eyes went directly to this: "It is not the nature of what you do that determines the spirituality of any action, but the origin of what you do."[1]

If what I do is done in complete dependence upon the Father, then it doesn't matter what that thing is, rather who the one is doing that thing. Is it me? Or is it him? Colossians says that by faith, it is beautifully and mysteriously both. "To this end I labor, struggling with all his energy, which so powerfully works in me" (Col. 1:29 NIV). Who am I to decide what is extraordinary? The Father has already decided. He says he himself is extraordinary. So anything I do as I depend on and partner with the Extraordinary One, I suppose that is extraordinary too.

Defending Martha: What She Got Right

Whenever we talk about biblical service, it seems Martha's name always comes up as an example of what not to do. Poor Martha. I often find myself becoming defensive of her, which should come as no surprise considering all the characteristics she and I have in common. Martha was vintage good girl. Before we pick apart all the things Martha did wrong, it is important to notice what she got right.

She welcomed Jesus in. "Now as they were traveling along, He entered a village; and a woman named Martha welcomed Him into her home" (Luke 10:38). Martha genuinely wanted to have him there. She didn't *have* to go out and ask him to come in. She was an eager hostess and willing to have guests even though the work wasn't done yet.

The Greek word used here for *welcomed* is also used later in Luke 19:5–6, when the Lord calls to a certain rich tax collector who climbed up a tree because he was too short to see over the crowd. "And [Jesus] said to him, 'Zacchaeus, hurry and come down, for I must stay at your house today.' So he hurried and came down and *received him joyfully*" (ESV).

Martha received the Lord joyfully, welcoming him with eagerness. Her motives started out right, as those of a good girl often do. She wanted to have him there.

She valued his company in the way she knew how. "Martha was distracted with all her preparations" (Luke 10:40). Knowing how the story ends, it is easy to say she was disrespecting the presence of Jesus by not paying him any attention. From her perspective, however, she was working because she knew how important this was. It wasn't because she didn't care. Perhaps it was because she cared so much. Still, her focus was misplaced.

She didn't hide when she got mad. "Lord, do You not care that my sister has left me to do all the serving alone? Then tell her to help me" (Luke 10:40). This is what I love about Martha and why, even though she had so much to learn about what intimacy with Jesus looks like, I believe she can also teach good girls a thing or two.

Martha didn't stay hidden behind her servant mask to suffer as a silent martyr. She could have faked happy until Jesus left and then blasted Mary for her lack of help. She could have given Mary the silent treatment for days after that gathering. There is nothing like a good dose of passive aggression toward a sister to get your point across. More, she could have kept all the anger and resentment to herself and then talked about Jesus behind his back, blaming him for allowing Mary to be lazy while she did all the work. That's probably what I would have done.

But Martha didn't do any of that. Instead, she immediately took her frustration to the one whom she knew could do something about it. "Lord, do You not care that my sister has left me to do all the serving alone?" And if that weren't brazen enough, she adds, "Then tell her to help me." It's bold, rash, and embarrassing. But at least she was being honest.

Still, Jesus honored Mary for her choice to sit with him, for her humble and reckless abandon to him. While I know he's right, the good girl in me stands rigid next to Martha with my hands on my hips. *That's great and all,* I say with her, *but who's gonna feed the people?*

With that, I reveal what I truly believe about God and service and my own role in his story. I see myself as irreplaceable when I think that the work won't get done unless I do it. Instead of looking to him to provide what is needed, Martha rolled up her sleeves and took on responsibility for things that may never have been meant for her.

Martha, Martha: Where She Went Wrong

Martha put natural limitations on a supernatural God. There were people in her home who were hungry and needed to eat. It wouldn't be right to let them starve. Perhaps she placed her interpretation of what the people needed above the Lord's. In her eyes, they needed food. Her knowledge of what happens when people get hungry outweighed her ability to imagine the impossible. She potentially missed out on watching a miracle because she was depending on herself to feed the people.

Think of how infertile Sarah in the Old Testament wanted a baby above everything else. Her human, finite knowledge of how babies are made compelled her to convince Abraham to conceive with Hagar. What if Mary, the mother of Jesus, put those same limitations on God? When the angel came to her and told her she would conceive a child and give birth to a son and call his name Jesus, imagine if she had freaked out and tried to make a baby in the normal way. Her simple trust in our supernatural God was the most important act of faith in history. "I am the Lord's servant," Mary answered. "May it be to me as you have said" (Luke 1:38 NIV).

I love that Mary uses the word *servant* here, because it communicates that service is an act of faith. It isn't me doing work for God, but it is me trusting God to do the work in me. That is what Mary did. She believed the angel, and then she offered herself as a servant. She didn't pull herself up and get to work. Instead, she ran to Elizabeth her cousin and began to sing. Worship, not work, flows out of the hearts of those who believe.

Martha's desire to please clouded her willingness to trust. I understand this mistake of Martha's perhaps more than any other. Given the choice to please God or to trust God, good girls become conflicted. We know we're supposed to trust God, but trust is so intangible. It almost seems passive in the face of all there is to do.

The authors of the book *TrueFaced* refer to this choice between pleasing God and trusting God as a fork in the road. "The marker leading to the left simply says Pleasing God. The one leading to the right reads Trusting God. It's hard to choose one over the other, because both roads have a good feel to them. We discover there is no third road and it becomes obvious that we will not be able to jump back and forth between the paths. We must choose one. *Only* one."[2] Martha chose to please him because trusting looked passive. To simply sit at his feet and do nothing bordered on offensive to this strong, capable woman. Martha was going to please God no matter what it took.

Martha tried to do *in order* to be. I don't believe Martha simply chose cooking or housework over the Lord. When she begged the Lord to make Mary help her, what she was really saying was "Notice me, Lord!" She wanted him to see her. She longed for acknowledgment and love, and was willing to do anything to get it. I imagine she could have been thinking *I wish I were able to sit at Jesus' feet like Mary. But I have to get this work done or the people won't eat.* It isn't that she *wanted* to be working. It's that she thought she had to. She felt responsible. And it wasn't fair. *Lord, tell her to help me!*

How Jesus Changes Everything

When Martha went over to tell Jesus her worries, begging him to notice her and all her efforts, he simply said her name. Twice. Gently, sweetly, reassuringly. "Martha, Martha. You are worried and bothered about so many things, but only one thing is necessary" (Luke 10:41–42 NASB).

A few years ago, I attended a conference where my sweet friend Renee Swope gave a talk based on her her book *A Confident Heart*.[3] She shared the story of Mary and Martha, and when she got to the part about Jesus' response to Martha's pleas, she simply asked the audience, "What are your many things?"

When I heard that, the tears were surprising and immediate. I thought to myself, *Oh girl. Do you have a week?* Because my many things list was deep and wide. It was the regular day things, like home keeping, food making, clothes washing, and children rearing. And at that particular moment, it was also the dream-wishing things, the stuff of later and someday all mixed in with right now. My many things list felt heavy and impossible. I had so many things.

And then Renee spoke of the choice we have to receive the gift of rest, because we have a God who sees and cares and notices. He will not come undone. He remains un-overwhelmable.

I wanted to stand up, clap, and whistle. I wanted to burst into the ugly cry. More, I wanted to give myself permission to sit down on the inside and live like I have a God who knows what he's doing.

"You are worried and bothered about so many things; but only one thing is necessary, for Mary has chosen the good part, which shall not be taken away from her" (Luke 10:41–42).

Choosing to please God sounds right at first, but it so often leads to a performing life, a girl trying to become good, a lean-on-myself theology. If I am trying to please God, it is difficult to trust God. But when I trust God, pleasing him is automatic.

Anything we do to get life and identity outside of Christ is an idol, even service to Christ. He doesn't want my service. He wants me. And from that life-giving relationship, "streams of living water will flow from within" (John 7:38 NIV).

So serve. By all means, serve. But don't do it from behind a martyr's mask of duty or self-righteous obligation. By faith, believe that you are free to do it from a place of total and complete acceptance by the only One who is extraordinary.

ᏋᏋ Behind the Mask ᏋᏋ

If I were Martha, I would have waited until Jesus left and then given Mary the silent treatment, only to finally blow up at her a few days later. What would you have done?

In what ways has your desire to please clouded your willingness to trust?

While talking about the story of Mary and Martha, my friend Jennifer said this: "I wish there was a third sister. Because what if you aren't working in the kitchen or sitting at Jesus' feet? What if you're asleep in the bedroom and you can't seem to get up?" In what ways are you like Martha? Mary? The invisible other sister?

What is on your many things list? Are you able to focus on the one thing, or are you always doing one *more* thing? What if you gave that list to Jesus for a day? What would that day look like?

6

······

the rule follower

hiding behind her spiritual disciplines

You are not under law, but under grace.
—Romans 6:14

*I*t was a hard day of first grade. No sooner did we arrive home from school than I realized I left my lunch box in the coat closet of my classroom. Which meant my banana peel was officially beginning to stink it all up. Which also meant I would have to take my lunch in a brown bag tomorrow. Which also meant people would notice that I had forgotten my lunch box in the coat closet. Which also meant that I would have to stoop down and rummage through fallen coats while looking for my lunch box tomorrow. Which somehow, in my six-year-old mind, seemed to mean that I was a bad person because I made a mistake.

It all sounds so ridiculous. I want to shout to my kid-self, "Lighten up!" But any failure to do as I was supposed to do was devastating to me, even in first grade. My mom finally convinced my friend Audra to find my lunch box for me the next day at school. I watched nervously from my desk as she happily bounced over to the coat closet to search for my lunch box, her scrawny legs folded up beneath her as she bent down to find that which belonged to me. Such freedom she had! It was a great relief not to have to do that myself. People wouldn't have to know I forgot my lunch box. People wouldn't have to know I made a mistake.

There are those who are hostile toward rules. They see rules as the enemy, like a prison warden with a whip and handcuffs. I get it. But as a good girl, I saw rules as more of a fickle friend. When I followed them and was able to keep them well, rules treated me right. They gave me guidelines to follow and keep, a measuring stick to let me know how I was doing. But those times when I couldn't measure up or I bent under the weight of them, those rules turned on me fast. They became burdensome and judgmental, a heavy, un-welcome enemy. I could never quite figure out how to make them like me *all* the time.

Still, I like knowing the rules. If the sign says Don't Touch, I don't touch. If it says Keep Out, I stay away. If the form is due on Friday, I'll turn it in on Thursday just in case. If the doctor says take one in the morning and one at night, I am sure to space them out exactly twelve hours. And even though I admit to occasionally bringing candy into the movie theater, I am always worried that the ticket person will search my bags and throw me out for smuggling in a bottle of water and two Peppermint Patties.

If the rules are ambiguous or not known, it's worse. I am nervous and hesitant to let my kids play on the school play-ground after school because I fear there may be a rule against that. I worry when I park on the street downtown if there is no meter. *Am I allowed to park here? Will I get a ticket?*

So you can imagine what happens when I break the rules, even when it is an accident. Sitting on a gurney in the hall of the hospital, I remember looking up at the police officer and asking him if I was going to jail. An hour earlier, I had been enjoying the sunny day, on my way to the mall to use a 20-percent-off coupon. While listening to Peter Gabriel sing "In Your Eyes," windows down, heart alive with hope that comes with springtime, I casually turned into the mall parking lot. I didn't see the car coming.

The accident was my fault, though the other driver got a ticket for driving too fast. I had never been in a car accident like this one: namely, one that was my fault. When you are a good girl who finds your identity in your performance, then mistakes mean punishment. So after riding to the hospital in an ambulance with the driver of the other car (who had a broken leg, by the way—oh the guilt!), I asked if I was going to jail. Because in my mind, people who cause car accidents are criminals and should be punished. And now I was one.

I will never forget the look of surprise and amusement on the police officer's face as he assured me I would not be going to jail. I will also never forget the relief.

Other parts of life where there are no rules at all, I become irritated and slightly irrational. Like on a long, lazy summer day when my kids want to play with the neighbors, I tend to hesitate calling because I don't want to bother them. There are no rules to tell me when it's okay to call my neighbors. Perhaps that is why I had such trouble allowing myself to be creative in my house when I was first married: *I didn't know the rules.* Creativity doesn't come with a rule book, but it seemed to me that Christianity did.

When Good Things Turn Bad

My senior year of high school, all the seniors in our youth group received a book from our youth pastor. Each chapter described a different spiritual discipline for the Christian life: prayer, Bible reading, journaling, evangelism, and so forth. By the time I headed off to my first year of Bible college, I had that book marked up in the best way. I had been a believer for ten years by now, so I thought I knew what it took to live the Christian life right. This book supported my bullet-point Jesus, and I was confidently on my way to becoming who God wanted me to be.

It's hard to write about this mask because the spiritual disciplines are good things. The problem is not the fact that we do them; it is our good-girl interpretation of what doing these things means. For many years, I lived as a believer in God but I did not live *from* God. I was a child of the God of grace but I was looking for life in the law.

Though I never would have admitted it had I been asked, my deepest belief was that I had to perform for God in order to earn his acceptance. I would try hard to muster up the motivation I thought was required of me to achieve it, but there was always a sense of desperation, frustration, and fear that perhaps I wasn't doing enough. That was the problem with my checklist theology: sometimes my list remained unchecked.

The mindset with which I typically approached my walk with God was one of attempting victory but secretly expecting defeat. If I prayed for ten minutes, I knew I could have prayed for twenty. If I read one chapter of Psalms, I wondered if I should have read two. I can't count how many New Year's Days I resolved to read through the entire Bible in a year because I was trying to satisfy the law I had in my head.

Occasionally, I was able to live up to the rules I thought God wanted me to follow. Then I would look down my nose at those who didn't or couldn't, while only a week later finding myself in their same condition, unable to perform anymore, defeated from all the effort. Instead of facing the failure and allowing the law to show me my need for a Savior, I consoled my failure with new and improved intentions to prove myself by myself. And the cycle continued.

Where is Christ in all of these rules and law-based beliefs? It's true that I experienced glimpses of rest and victory, but those generally came only after a long period of what I considered to be acceptable obedience. Rarely, if ever, did I experience rest simply because I knew I was loved with an everlasting love by my Creator. My personal truth was *I have to be perfect. And when I'm not, I have to pay.* In a way, I was right. The law does indeed require perfection. And breaking the law demands payment. So the question remains: Why did God give the law if we can never measure up to it?

The Real Purpose of the Law

Since the fall in Genesis 3, humankind has had a heart condition. This heart condition is not merely a lack of sincerity or motivation. It is not a bent toward rebellion or an obstacle to be overcome with better performance or new resolutions. "And you were dead in your trespasses and sins, in which you formerly walked according to the course of this world, according to the prince of the power of the air, of the spirit that is now working in the sons of disobedience. Among them we too all formerly lived in the lusts of our flesh, indulging the desires of the flesh and of the mind, and were by nature children of wrath, even as the rest" (Eph. 2:1–3).

That's bad. No amount of try-hard good intentions can fix that mess. But as a good girl, those verses are hard to relate with. I never remember a time when that could have described me, really: trespasses and sins, sons of disobedience, lusts of the flesh, children of wrath. Are you kidding me? A girl afraid of a parking ticket does not go around in the lusts of her flesh. I accepted Jesus when I was young and never did the really bad stuff.

But this passage is not just talking about my behavior. It is referring to my identity. And without Christ, it says I was dead. We were born enemies of the living God as a result of the fall. (We'll talk more about that in chapter 10.) If I had continued in my dead state, the result would have been me walking in the lusts of my flesh. That looks

71

different for everyone, but it is always bad and it is always based on self.

Man without God is totally without hope. As if this isn't problem enough, there is yet another obstacle: man *did not know* he was totally without hope. Prior to the law, man was born unaware of his condition before God. So God decided to make us aware of our heart problem. A person won't seek help until they are aware of their need. The way God chose to reveal this heart problem has always seemed strange and cruel to me. But since I have come to know and understand his grace, I have been awed to discover that his giving the law to humankind was nothing short of another gracious, magnificent act in human history.

Exodus 19 begins the account of Moses receiving the law from God. When Moses descended from that mountain and stated God's requirements for its fulfillment, the people all responded together: "All that the LORD has spoken we will do!" (19:8). Oh, the irony in that statement. Moses went back up the mountain to hear the details, and the rules went on for four chapters, all of the requirements of the law. Again, when Moses came down and told the people all of the Lord's words and laws, they responded with one voice, "All the words which the LORD has spoken we will do!" (Exod. 24:3).

With what power did they expect to be able to fulfill the requirements of a holy God? Just reading the details of the law makes me want to take a nap. Still, I hear myself in their response. *Yes, Lord! I will be careful to do everything you require!*

His law reveals his character in external form: perfection. He is perfect, so his law is perfect. And there is that word again. But the people believed that if they tried hard enough, surely they could fulfill the requirements needed to please God. History reveals they could not. The law was designed to expose our heart condition, to make us see our guilt. It was never meant to make us righteous. "Therefore no one will be declared righteous in his sight by observing the law;

rather, through the law we become conscious of sin" (Rom. 3:20 NIV).

I've heard several pastors and teachers over the years compare the law to a mirror. If I have dirt on my face, I go to the mirror and it shows me the truth. The mirror isn't bad; it simply reveals what is there. At the same time, the mirror by itself has no power to clean my face. It would be foolish to take the mirror from the wall and rub my face with it, trying to clean off the dirt. But that is what good girls do with the law. We believe that by keeping it, we will somehow gain favor.

So why would a holy God give an impossible standard to a group of born failures who, no matter how sincere or how dedicated or how determined, could never, ever live up to it? God should have known we couldn't fulfill those expectations. But the secret of the law was not to prove our inadequacy for God's sake. It was to prove our inadequacy for our sake.

The Mask of Law, the Face of Grace

God longs for us to place our trust in him rather than in ourselves. One way to do that was to give us a law we could not keep to show us how very perfect he is. And there, in our weak and helpless condition, we would finally agree with him. We need someone to act on our behalf. And so he did. "Therefore the Law has become our tutor to lead us to Christ, so that we may be justified by faith" (Gal. 3:24). A tutor leads the student to the source and power of the truth. The tutor is not, by himself, enough. "But now a righteousness from God, apart from law, has been made known, to which the Law and the Prophets testify. This righteousness from God comes through faith in Jesus Christ to all who believe" (Rom. 3:21–22 NIV).

The law was given to lead the unbeliever to her Savior, not for the believer to try to keep it. "The Law is holy, and the commandment is holy and righteous and good" (Rom. 7:12). Without the standard, we would never be aware of our desperate need. Law in the life of a believer will do the same thing it is designed to do in the life of a nonbeliever: lead her to the end of her own resources.

The law is based on principles and standards to live up to, but the life of the Spirit is based on a promise. Striving characterizes the law whereas rest characterizes grace. The law places responsibility on me to do, but grace is given by the initiative of God and invites me to be. Trying to keep the law leads to bondage, forcing me to figure things out on my own and cower behind a mask when I can't get it right. But the grace of God brings freedom and power to do as he wills. Under the law, I struggle in vain attempts to control my behavior. Under grace, my life is an easy expression of the Spirit. The law says obey. Grace says believe and obedience will follow.

In a sermon series simply titled *Grace*, Dudley Hall says this about the law: "Grace is not Jesus helping you live up to the law. This keeps us focused on the law. Jesus came to fulfill the law so we don't have to look at it anymore. I no more listen to what the law is saying, I listen to what Jesus is saying."[1]

The mask of the spiritual disciplines is one of the hardest to put down for the good girl who has been living according to the law. The reason we hide is because we fear if we come out from behind it, we won't be enough. And the truth is, apart from Christ, we won't. We believe we have to be competent in ourselves, forgetting God's truth. I love how Paul speaks directly to that fear of inadequacy in 2 Corinthians 3:4–6: "Not that we are competent in ourselves to claim anything for ourselves, but our competence comes from God. He has made us competent as ministers of a new covenant—not of the letter but of the Spirit; for the letter kills, but the Spirit gives life" (NIV).

This Jesus-dependent life is not a balance between a little bit of law and a little bit of grace. Be sure not to tip too far to one side! That's the problem: we can't figure how to keep the scale balanced all the time. The true gospel says we don't have to.

As good girls, we are so used to hearing words like *you ought to, you should,* and *you must.* With those same ears, we try to listen to Jesus and it sounds as though he speaks the same language. But that is the language of the law. It is time to say goodbye to fake, ought-to Jesus and meet the real one.

Lynne Hybels knows about fake Jesus. She and her husband Bill started Willow Creek Community Church in 1975. A self-described "nice girl," Lynne details a time in her life when she had to turn her back on the God of her childhood, the God who demanded too much, required too much, and basically sucked the life out of her. "As the ultimate nice girl and striver after divine favor, it was no small thing to turn my back on God. I didn't broadcast this decision. I was still a pastor's wife. I didn't want to confuse people or shake anyone else's faith, but I was done with a God who daily sucked the life out of me—and I was too tired to search for a replacement."[2]

What really happened, she continues to explain, is that the Spirit of the true God gave her the courage to let go of the fake one. And in his presence is where she found rest, healing, and security.

A Better Hope

Though my dad is an alcoholic, he has been sober for over twenty years. In fact, after he accepted Jesus when I was eleven, he quickly became the first person I thought of when I needed wisdom, direction, or perspective. He is to me a right picture of a father on earth, a present reflection of what a father's love is meant to be. I have had the privilege of watching the difference Jesus makes in a person's life. I watched my dad go from a defeated, passive, there-but-not-there shadow man to a vibrant, passionate, loving, alive, present man.

Only Jesus does things like that.

Talking about spiritual disciplines, my dad told me that there is a difference between the discipline of sitting down with God and the pleasure of knowing his voice. It is one thing to make yourself do something. It is entirely another to find pleasure in relationship. "The former regulation is set aside because it was weak and useless (for the law made nothing perfect), and a better hope is introduced, by which we draw near to God" (Heb. 7:18–19 NIV).

To wear the mask of the spiritual disciplines is to turn back to the old way. I could pray for five minutes or for two days and I would still be as righteous as I would be had I not prayed at all. But the amazing reality is that now that I know I am righteous in Christ, there is new motivation to spend time in intimate communion. You and I can now go to him in freedom and joy, not to gain favor but because we already have it. We are free to draw near rather than to try to please from afar.

I love the way Dudley Hall says it: "When you get miserable enough to die, you can be free. Go ahead and live under the law—give it your best shot. Ultimately the law will make you so miserable, you'll want to die. Then you will find that someone already died for you."[3]

✎ Behind the Mask ✎

Living as a good girl, my personal truth was *I have to be perfect or I have to pay.* Can you define a similar statement you have lived by in your own life?

Do you see rules as friend, foe, or a mix of both?

What is the difference between living *for* God and living *from* God?

In what ways might you be trying to please a fake, ought-to Jesus?

Consider Romans 10:4 (NIV): "Christ is the end of the law so that there may be righteousness for everyone who believes." Are you willing to receive that righteousness, or are you still trying to work hard to earn it? Does this gift feel freeing or offensive to you?

7

can't fall apart

hiding behind her strength and responsibility

I'm always the strong one, the one who helps. I don't think
people assume I'm struggling. Ever.
                                        —Deb, a recovering good girl

*G*oing to hell was not an option. I was seven when my
mom sat me down and told me of the reality of heaven
and hell, Jesus and sin. When I learned where she would
be going, I decided heaven was the place for me. Wherever
Mommy went, that's where I wanted to be, too.

As I said before, my dad didn't know Jesus when I was little.
He was a passive alcoholic who came home late from work
and fell asleep on the floor. I loved my dad. I didn't always
understand how to be myself around him, but I remember
wanting his acceptance more than anyone else's.

I prayed for him to accept Jesus more than I prayed for
anything. Not only that, I made wishes. Every time I saw a

red bird or a falling star, or threw a penny in a fountain, I would wish for my dad to accept Jesus. Sometimes I'd wish for a ten-speed bike, but whatever.

My dad quit drinking when I was still young. There was no fanfare, no come-to-Jesus moment, and no support group. He simply quit. Knowing what I now know about alcoholism, that fact is nothing short of a miracle. Not only that, he began to show slight interest in the Bible and would occasionally go to church with us instead of staying home alone and listening to Bruce Springsteen loud on his record player. I dared not hope for him to accept Jesus until one afternoon in our suburban Iowa basement, he asked me to tell him a Bible story.

This is it! I thought to myself. *This is my chance! Make it good, Emily. Make. It. Good.* I blanked. I had nothing. Visions of flannel graphs, Kool-Aid, and lemon-flavored cookies flew through my mind, memories from VBS and Sunday school. But a Bible story? A complete, bona fide Jesus story that would lead my dad into eternal life with God? I wasn't prepared! Why hadn't I prepared? It was a lot of pressure for an eleven-year-old.

Just then, a familiar little tune weaved its way to the surface and before I could stop myself, out it came.

"Zacchaeus was a wee little man. A wee little man was he." It was the best I could do. I tried to say it nonchalant-like. I tried to hide the fact that it rhymed. *Maybe he won't notice it's a song.*

"He climbed up in a sycamore tree for the Lord he wanted to see." Dad didn't say much after that; merely smiled and nodded his head. I walked up the stairs to my room feeling overwhelmed with the weight of my dad's eternal destiny, kicking myself for choosing such an idiotic, childish Bible story about a short dude in a crowd.

It wasn't long after that day in the basement when my alcoholic dad accepted Jesus as his personal Savior, no thanks to me and Zacchaeus. Yet, the story is significant to illustrate the point: *I felt responsible for my dad's salvation.*

When Good Things Turn Bad

Being strong and responsible are not bad things. Paying the bills is the responsible thing to do. Being honest, loving your kids, driving the speed limit, and doing the dishes: all responsible choices. These things are not what I'm referring to as the mask of responsibility. This definition of the word gives a better idea of what the mask looks like.

> re·spon·si·ble: liable to be called on to answer; liable to be called to account as the primary cause, motive, or agent; being the cause or explanation[1]

It means taking things on as my own that were never meant for me to take on. It is the false belief that I, myself, am *the cause or explanation* for the bad, uncomfortable, or dissatisfied people or circumstances around me. Likewise, it also means that I feel the need to prevent the bad, uncomfortable, or dissatisfactory circumstances from happening in the first place.

I can't remember a time when I didn't feel responsible. I was responsible to be right. I was responsible to look good. I was responsible to have it all together. I was responsible for being responsible. Just now at the coffee shop, the barista asked if I would like my chocolate chip cookie heated up. And I did. But I said no because I felt responsible for the extra work it would take for her to do so.

I walk into a room and if someone has a scowl on their face, I think I have to fix it. If people in my family aren't getting along, I feel the weight of it and believe it is my job to do something about it. But it's double-edged, this weight of responsibility. For all the times I rush around, both physically and mentally, trying to fix and influence the people and circumstances around me, I simultaneously feel resentful that I am the one to manage it all. *Why doesn't anyone else fix this? Why do I have to be the one?* Even though I was the one who wrote the job description and hired myself to fill the role, I want to both quit and fire myself.

I am never satisfied with me.

There are bigger things that come from this inflated sense of responsibility. People go their entire lives carrying the burden of blame for things over which they had no control: the death of a friend, their parents' divorce, car accidents, and natural disasters.

But what about those things where it seems we have some control? It's those blurry things that trip me up, the things that perhaps I could have changed or had some type of influence in the outcome. Those decisions are the ones that paralyze me, causing me to constantly question if I'm doing enough, saying just the right thing, and handling life the way I ought to be. I don't want to carry the heavy load of responsibility, but when I'm wearing this mask, I don't see any other option.

On Being Responsible

Several years ago, my friend Faith and I decided to visit New York City to celebrate her thirtieth birthday. Some girlfriends of ours had an apartment in Brooklyn, and we were looking forward to a few days of girly fun.

One night before dinner, we decided to ride one of the horse-drawn carriages through Central Park. As soon as I got into that carriage, the first thing I did was plop my heavy bag onto the seat next to me. I never once considered keeping that bag strapped to my shoulder for the ride. I never once thought of carrying the bag myself so the horse wouldn't have to. That would be a weird and crazy thing to do.

The amount of crazy it would take for a girl on a carriage ride to keep the bag strapped to her shoulder is equal to the amount of crazy I am when I refuse to trust the Lord to handle my worries.

Jesus says in Matthew 11:28, "Come to Me, all who are weary and heavy-laden, and I will give you rest." Rest from carrying heavy loads, heavy burdens, and unrealistic responsibilities. We can go to Jesus with those worries, because only he can handle them anyway.

But he carries more than my burdens. Not only was that carriage already carrying my bag, the carriage was carrying me, which is infinitely more important. God doesn't ask us to be strong. In fact, I believe the Bible teaches that he asks us to be the exact opposite.

The Purse

My friend Kelly knows firsthand about the insatiable need of the good girl to be strong and to be needed. By the time she was in the sixth grade, Kelly realized how it was natural for people to respond to her when she had something they needed. So she came up with the idea of "The Purse." Here is her story, in her own words.

> I was never one for the popular crowd. I would do almost anything for the approval of people, particularly the people who insisted on rejecting me. I needed to find something to win friends. So, I came up with the idea of The Purse. I packed tissues, highlighters, pens, pencils, gum, paper, journals, erasers, makeup remover, spare change, ChapStick, you-name-it into granny-size purses for years, just so that I could have whatever someone needed when they needed it.
>
> As I became more style-conscious, I downsized my purse, but The Purse mentality carried over into my life. I would go the extra mile to serve in church. I'd sing if there was no one else to do it. I'd play the piano—weddings, funerals, church services—unpaid. I'd babysit for free, every time. People took advantage of me, but I didn't mind. I felt loved if they asked my help again.
>
> But my freshman year of college, I dropped The Purse. I couldn't carry it anymore. It was too heavy for me. Others stepped in to meet needs that I couldn't meet. I hadn't been building relationship, and the people I helped weren't seeking it. So I was left alone.

Need meeting isn't always love, and it is love that fills us up, that nourishes relationship, that changes a life. I am only beginning to understand that.[2]

Can you imagine a high school student carrying around all that stuff everywhere she went? I love how Kelly makes the connection between the physical purse she carried and the mental one that continued long after she put down the real purse. When I'm in hiding, I constantly carry a purse in my mind, filling it with ways to find my worth in people. What looks like strength on the outside is actually a deep, cavernous well of neediness.

The Mask Revealed

Ten years before our New York trip, Faith and I met at my sister's wedding. I was the maid of honor and she was the guest book attendant. I was immediately drawn to her just as my sister said I would be. By night's end, we had agreed to be roommates the following year. She was a year older than me, so she already had a year of college behind her, a fact that somehow brought me confidence by association going into my freshman year.

She was fun and funny, playful and vivacious, blonde and gorgeous. She was dramatic, jealous, passionate, and by the standards of our small Bible college in South Carolina, she could be downright scandalous.

It was little things that bonded us at first—we wore the same size shoes and could share clothes and both had an unnatural love for our favorite musicals. But we shared a lot more than just a room during those years in college. We shared dreams and drama, heartache and heartbreaks, as well as a love for the Lord.

But for all the ways Faith and I were alike, there were ten times the ways in which we were different. I kept my desk clean and organized. She would sit on her bed and chat with me while I cleaned out hers, too. I would worry about the rules. She would break the ones that didn't matter so much. I avoided confrontation and smiled no matter what. She walked confidently ahead and bravely shook hands with controversy while wearing a mischievous grin on her pretty face, a twinkle in her bright green eyes.

Rooming with Faith was perhaps the first time I became aware of my mask of strength and responsibility. Until that first year of college, I was able to remain safely hidden behind it, unaware of the ways in which I kept my own truth tucked away. Faith wouldn't wait for me to ask how she was doing. She would simply talk, cry, share, and live freely in front of me. I would watch her and wonder how she could be so vulnerable. There were even times when I felt resentment toward her. *Why doesn't she care about how I'm doing? Why are we always talking about her stuff?*

The truth was, she did care. And she did ask. But because I hid behind this mask, I wasn't really able to articulate my stuff, so I would find ways to turn it back to her, to deflect the spotlight, to avoid the questions. In my silence and refusal to be vulnerable, I inadvertently taught her that I had no needs, no weakness, and no reason to lean on her.

I have spent most of my life avoiding weak. I don't want to look weak, act weak, or even give the hint that I am capable of weakness. But if *you* are feeling weak? Well, now. That's a different thing altogether. I can tell you how weakness is the door to strength and how Jesus calls us to a life of weakness so that he can be strong. And I believe it. For you.

For the girl who wears the mask of strength and responsibility, it is important to explore her perceptions of weakness. Consider what Jesus says about weakness. He chose the foolish things of the world to shame the wise and the weak things of the world to shame the strong (1 Cor. 1:27). It doesn't make sense to me and it isn't the way I'd have done it. But it is the way of Jesus.

He talks about how his grace is enough and about how weakness is the pathway to experiencing his strength. And

Paul, the man who had more good-boy points than any other man in the Bible, delighted in his own weaknesses for Christ's sake. "For when I am weak, then I am strong" (2 Cor. 12:10).

"Weak" is not a four-letter bad word. Hiding behind a mask of strength and responsibility is a lonely place to live. That mask portrays to the world around us that we have it all together, that we can handle the mess, that we don't need people, or worse, that we don't need God.

Ragamuffin Good Girls

Brennan Manning is the author of one of my favorite books, *Reflections for Ragamuffins*. He says there is more power in sharing our weaknesses than our strengths. As a good girl, I have a hard time with that one, especially if it means other people might think I don't know everything or that I don't have it all together. The truth is, admitting weakness is the very doorway the Lord uses to lead the tired good girl to a place of rest.

Two years ago, my friend Kendra and I began noticing this mask-wearing addiction among the girls in our youth group. It was easy to spot, as both Kendra and I have spent the better part of our lives living behind the mask of strength and responsibility. We decided to take action and organize an extended time for some of these girls to hang out together and chat it up about Jesus, life, and the masks we hide behind.

We chose a Saturday in January to invite the good girls for an overnight gabfest. There were twenty high school seniors hanging out on my living room floor, forty eyes darting around wondering if it was safe to come out from behind the mask. As we began to share with them our own messy stories of trying to measure up, of failing to trust Jesus, and of longing to be free, the air in the room shifted from reserved to relaxed. Then, it happened. One brave girl stepped out

85

from behind her well-worn mask to share things she feared and ways she struggled. Heads nodded all around, tears collectively threatened to spill over from understanding eyes, and the girls began to trust each other.

We couldn't have stopped them from sharing with each other even if we had wanted to, because Brennan Manning is right: *There is more power in sharing our weaknesses than our strengths.*

Trust Transplant

The power doesn't stop there. If you are anything like me, then you know the fine art of how to be vulnerable enough so people believe you are authentic, but not so vulnerable that all your mess hangs out. You know how to be vulnerable with boundaries. Even though it is freeing and relieving to share our weakness with one another, that alone won't bring much relief in the long run.

Once we admit we can't manufacture circumstances, manage everyone's opinion of us, or be the all-knowing counselor, then we will be eager to transfer our trust in ourselves to trusting in another. We may be able to hide some of the mess with each other, but we have a God who sees and knows and loves no matter what. He is a generous, patient, compassionate God and his expectations of us are not the same as our expectations of ourselves.

Matthew 11:28 is Jesus' invitation for the weary and heavy-laden girl to come to him, but the invitation doesn't stop there. He continues in the following verses by saying, "Take My yoke upon you and learn from Me, for I am gentle and humble in heart, and you will find rest for your souls. For My yoke is easy and My burden is light" (Matt. 11:29–30).

That invitation is hard for this good girl to resist. I am in desperate need of someone to depend on other than myself. I need a trust transplant. How about you?

⤳ BEHIND THE MASK ⤳

In what ways do you take responsibility for things unnecessarily? In what ways are you trying to manage outcomes from behind your mask of responsibility?

Can you relate with Kelly's purse? In what ways do you need-meet for those around you?

Are you in the habit of teaching people you have no needs? How does it feel when they believe you?

What comes to mind when you hear the word *weak*? Is it a person? A point in time? A feeling? A memory?

Compare your idea of weak with 2 Corinthians 12:10: "For when I am weak, then I am strong."

8

picket fences

hiding behind her comfort zone

I struggle to be me . . . I bend myself into the right shape that
pleases everyone else.

—Dee, an experienced good girl

*I*f I could have gotten a job where my only responsibility was to watch people, I would likely have
climbed the corporate ladder at record speed. I could be
the CEO of the National People Watching Corporation.
And I would put my glass office in the middle of an airport
terminal. Or a coffee shop. Or a college campus. Really
anywhere would do.

I justify my stalker-ish tendencies by the fact that I learn
a lot about life by simply watching it happen around me. In
fact, one of my most self-aware moments happened on a
Tuesday afternoon in the children's section of a bookstore.

A Choice

The little girl wanted the pencils. I could tell right away. Her daddy sat near her, his long legs bent awkwardly to fit on the too-small chair. I watched them with stranger's eyes, slowly browsing a shelf nearby. She was deciding between a small, educational activity book or a set of colorful princess pencils. With the book in one hand and the pencils in the other, she quietly held them up to her daddy's face as if to ask him which one he thought she should choose.

He repeatedly told her it was her decision and she was free to choose either one. No sooner had the words come out of his mouth than he was giving her a list of pros and cons about each potential choice:

The pencils are pretty, but the *activity book* might last longer.

The pencils have to be sharpened and then they get smaller and smaller and eventually disappear.

The *activity book* has pages and pages of endless fun.

"But the choice is yours to make," he was sure to add on to the end.

I smiled to myself as I noticed his inability to remain uninvolved. It was obvious to me which one she would choose after his comments. *What five-year-old would choose the pretty pencils after Daddy clearly explained how impractical they were?*

I missed what happened next as I noticed my own girls had pulled nearly every board book from the shelf below me. I was glad for the distraction as it helped me maintain my cover.

When I looked up again, the man and his daughter stood to leave. As they passed me by, I noticed her satisfied expression and the pack of princess pencils in her small hand. I'm embarrassed to admit how surprised I was.

In that moment, I realized that no matter how much I may have wanted them, I *never* would have chosen the pencils. As a kid, I was too concerned about making the "right" choice, the choice that would please the most people. I did not give myself permission to make the fun choice when the outcome didn't matter.

I still do that a lot. I weigh, I consider, I balance and reconsider. I obsess over what they would do, what he would want, or what she would think of me. It is easy to blame it on responsibility or grown-up-ness or consequences, or to claim it as wisdom and experience.

But I think it has more to do with fear.

Watching that small, brave girl choose the pencils that day, I realized how my need to keep everyone happy with me has become a mask I hide behind in order to avoid risk and rejection. It feels comfortable there; comfortable enough to disregard the uneasy wave that sometimes rolls over me in the midst of it.

Sissy's Story

My friend Sissy learned the art of hiding her true self early in her marriage. Charlie and Sissy dated only a few months before they decided to get married. They felt instantly connected and knew God had brought them together, but Sissy admits to knowing nothing about how to be a wife.

Her idea of being the good wife meant a hot dinner every night when he came home, keeping a neat house, and washing his clothes.

She also believed she was supposed to form her opinions around his. She loved peas but wouldn't cook them because she knew he didn't like them. She waited for Charlie to come home for dinner before she would eat. Even if he called ahead to tell her to start without him, she refused and suffered through hunger headaches for the sake of being wifely.

"It was a year or two before he commented on how much I'd changed. He wondered where the spunky girl he dated was, the one who had an opinion on lots of different things. But I liked, and still like, to avoid conflict, so I would just not bring up anything that I thought would bring on conflict." She hid behind her peaceful comfort zone, which really wasn't so peaceful after all.

Eventually, Charlie shared with Sissy how he liked the fact that she had her own opinions about things. She admits to being confused about who she was, how to act, what to say. She admits to holding on tightly to this false identity she had created for fear of what might happen if she let it go.

"It took me a long time to take the mask off and really come back to being who I am underneath. At times we still struggle with me not wanting to tell him what I think. I tend to tell him in the important things, but if I'm not really concerned with it, if it doesn't affect me, I might tell him what he wants to hear."

And that is how it goes, until he confronts her about something. And when he does, she pulls out her list. Perhaps you know the list. It is the one filled with all those things that bother you that you haven't dared bring up, the things you have been saving for such a time as this. It is your defense list, your ammunition for protection. Because if you don't bring up your list, then all you are left with is someone telling you you've disappointed them, and a good girl doesn't like to be wrong or disappoint people. And so, we pull out our list and point back. It isn't pretty, but isn't it familiar?

Anatomy of a Mask

These stories point to the same intricately tangled root: fear. Our comfort zone is a widely drawn circle and we stand in the middle, protected by our ability to please everyone else, no matter the cost. We watch people from behind this not-so-secure comfort zone. We observe and interpret reactions through our own messed-up filters so that whatever is going on with others ultimately comes back around to us.

We master the art of asking insightful questions and become interested in others' lives because deep down we believe they are more important. And not in a Jesus kind of way, but

91

in a woe-is-me kind of way. We become skilled at getting to know people and have several who think of us as their closest friend, only to discover at the end of the day, we have no one to call because we're unwilling to trust. We deflect the threat of closeness by learning to read others' responses to us. In this, we simultaneously avoid and long for discovery.

If you are hiding behind your comfort zone, chances are that moving toward others is easy. You will help others, serve others, and pray for them, too. But there is a distinct possibility that if they begin to ask questions, you will move quickly on and deeply inward. You retreat to your comfortable living room behind the wreath-wearing front door of a well-built house with its white picket fence.

And you will smile and wave from a distance, because who they think you are is infinitely more important than who you really are.

Or, perhaps you don't even bother moving toward others, because in so doing, you put yourself at risk. They might not receive you well. They might turn you away. They might not be safe. And so you stay put.

You feel lonely, unimportant, and not-as-good-as, while at the same time you experience feelings of deep resentment toward those who always turn to you. You have trained people to think you have no needs, but you are secretly angry with them for believing you.

To Be Close

The Bible is filled with people who had to get close in order to be healed. In Mark 5:21, Jesus was surrounded by a great multitude of people, crowds of commoners wanting to see this God-man in action. A man named Jairus pushed his way through the crowd toward Jesus, desperate for him to perform a miracle.

When he saw Jesus, he fell at his feet, pleading. "My little daughter is at the point of death; please come and lay Your hands on her, so that she will get well and live" (Mark 5:23). Jairus wasn't just any man; he was a synagogue official, a very important, respected position. But that day in front of Jesus, he was just a frantic, worried father.

The crowd was large and people were pressing in and slowing down the Healer and the desperate father. And just when it seems the story has a plot rising to action with the dying girl as the primary character, a bleeding woman shows up. She had been bleeding for twelve years, and not only could no one heal her, they couldn't even tell her what was wrong.

She spent all her money to discover a cure, but her illness only grew worse. In that time, a bleeding woman was considered unclean and was not to be touched. The woman knew this and she didn't want to be a bother; she only wanted to be well. This Jesus was her last hope. In an attempt to remain anonymous and safely hidden among the crowd, she approached Jesus from behind and touched his cloak, knowing that would be enough. She had great faith but little self-esteem. She felt both desperate and invisible.

"Immediately the flow of her blood was dried up; and she felt in her body that she was healed of her affliction. Immediately Jesus, perceiving in Himself that the power proceeding from Him had gone forth, turned around in the crowd and said, 'Who touched My garments?'" (Mark 5:29–30).

She didn't speak up right away. In fact, she waited long enough for the disciples to silently roll their eyes at him and point out the huge crowd of people all around. Of course people were touching him! Everyone was touching everyone. How could he expect to identify one solitary touch? Healing always brings out the skeptics.

But Jesus continued to look around for her.

That must have been when she realized she had to identify herself. As much as she wanted to, she could not go unnoticed. "But the woman fearing and trembling, aware of what had happened to her, came and fell down before Him, and told Him the whole truth" (Mark 5:33). No more hiding in the crowd. No more trying to sneak in healing from a distance. It was time for her to be seen. And so she told him the whole truth. She stepped out from behind her comfort zone and fell at the feet of Jesus.

His response to her was both loving and life-giving. He calls her daughter, says her faith has made her well, and instructs her to go in peace, being healed of her affliction. Can you imagine the day she had after that face-to-face encounter with Jesus?

While he was still speaking with this newly healed woman, the very important synagogue official's young daughter passed from life into death. I can't help but wonder if the bleeding woman stuck around long enough to hear about the young girl. Even though Jesus knew this little girl was close to death, he still took the time to find the woman who touched his garments, to see her, to speak to her, and to make her whole.

His timing and lack of panic in the midst of great need amazes me, as does his ability to see and know and love without boundaries. Even death wouldn't stop him. He told Jairus not to be afraid but to believe. And he told a weeping crowd that the girl was merely sleeping. Their weeping turned to sarcastic laughter; the skeptics didn't believe. So he made them leave, with only the girl's parents and his closest disciples remaining.

Then, he took the girl's hand and simply said to her, "Get up!" And so she did.

Both of these were so dearly loved by Jesus, the sick woman and the dying girl. To be healed, there had to be a touch. And for a touch, they had to be close. Hiding behind a comfortable zone of perceived safety is not an option. Good girls are no exception.

Taking the Risk: What Will They Think of Me?

I shared the pencil story with my favorite online community, the women of (in)courage.[1] When I asked them if they would have chosen the pencils or the activity book, here are a few of their answers:

Carrie: "I fear and obsess, too, sadly. I would have chosen the activity book and later mourned my lack of assertiveness."

Christy: "Without a doubt I would have asserted my independence . . . inside my head, and then, driven by guilt and misery, would have placed both back."

Deidra: "I would not have asked my dad for his opinion. The choice would have been totally mine. And that is oh-so-similar to my relationship with my heavenly Father. I'm working on it. But it's not my natural bent to ask Him what He thinks."

Brianna: "I would have chosen the book and then flaunted the fact that I chose wisely to my sister who would have, no doubt, chosen the pencils."

Karen: "I think I probably would have chosen the book. I have been learning a lot in the last couple of years how most of my life has been lived in fear of being criticized, ridiculed, thought less of . . . you name it. I have just begun to recognize those moments in my life and am beginning to figure out which thoughts and feelings are truly mine and which are those I think will make others happy or help avoid conflict."

Isn't it fascinating how the choice of one small, brave girl in a bookstore on a Tuesday can inspire an entire community of women to reexamine the way we make decisions? I have missed out on a lot of freedom because of my fear of rejection. We may call it "people pleasing," but it is entirely self-serving because it is really all about keeping myself comfortable. Boiled down, it could be more accurately called "me pleasing."

When I'm wearing a mask, not only can others not see me, but I can't see them. I see everything through a thin veil of my own perception. I hide behind comfortable so that when I enter a room, I am unable to move toward people with interest because I am too concerned with what they are thinking of me. What would it look like if I allowed Jesus himself to determine my comfort zone? What if, instead of walking into a room with a wall around me, I was able to walk into a room and move toward others in freedom? Before I am able to do that, I have to be convinced I am safe. And that is exactly what Jesus came to do.

⟳ BEHIND THE MASK ⟳

Which would you have chosen: the pencils or the activity book? What factors determine the choices you make?

Are you able to relate with the desperation and insecurities of the bleeding woman in the crowd from Mark 5?

In what ways might you be hiding behind your comfort zone?

9

when it gets ugly

hiding behind her indifference

My life was tidy once. I was pretending.
—Kelly, a recovering good girl

*W*e were late. The line to catch the monorail was at
least a mile long, and our mini Snow White and
Sleeping Beauty were giddy with Disney energy. We nearly
missed our appointment for breakfast at the Castle, but a
few key people had compassion on us and we were able to
get there just in time.

As we shuffled our way through the doors, we peeled off
coats and hats from our little princess girls, the only downside
of Disney in January. They stood on tennis-shoed tiptoes,
eyebrows raised, searching for a glimpse of a glass-slippered,
blue-dressed princess with blonde hair piled high. We saw her
almost immediately and waited as other little princess girls
stood beside her, posing for photos. Then, it was our turn.

I watched as my self-professed anti-princess daughter stared up at Cinderella with delight. She watched Cinderella's every move, from the graceful way she beckoned her near to the sweet, gentle way of her voice. She quietly stayed close, sparkly fabric and blue tulle brushing her face as she stood waist-high to the grown-up princess.

I saw that actress playing Cinderella through my tired grown-girl eyes. And though I was thankful for her sugary act for the sake of my daughters, my inner cynic began a silent dialogue. It's easy to be Cinderella in the ball gown, the one who got the man, the one for whom everything worked out so beautifully, the one who had enemies safely avenged.

What about the Cinderella in the rags? In the movie, those big-footed stepsisters were rotten to her, and still she sang and was nice to mice and had pretty hair and was still skinny even in the midst of all that pressure. And she had to scrub floors and miss royal balls and churn butter out of mud.

What a sweet girl she was, but I can't help wondering, *What if I was Cinderella in the rags?* I would be hopping mad by the time that ball rolled around. I may have been able to hide it for a while, but the mistreatment and the unfairness of it all would have eaten away at me until I exploded.

As if that weren't bad enough, I wonder what would have happened if those stepsisters got to meet princes, too? What if they had been whisked away and had special glass slippers just like Cinderella? What then? That would not have been okay with me. If I were Cinderella, I would have thrown that glass shoe directly at Anastasia and hoped it further ruined her already ugly face. *No fair!* I would shout. *They don't deserve the prince! I DO!*

Good girls are a lot like my rag-wearing Cinderella.

Because if you are working in your own strength, then who gets the credit?

You do.

If you aren't being rewarded for your hard work, who gets offended?

98

You do.

If things aren't going the way they should, who gets angry? You guessed it.

Sometimes I am this way with Jesus. Even though I know the Bible says I am not saved by my works but by faith, I still believe deep down that God is more accepting of those who perform well and do the right things than he is of those who do not. And I believe that the bad girls shouldn't get the same rewards that the good girls get. It's only fair.

So Cinderella? She wins. Stepsisters? They lose. But that is not how salvation works. And it's not how walking with Jesus works, either.

Straight from My Ugly

I have some beautiful friends who are being used mightily by the Lord. Some are single, others are married, and a few are divorced. They have all experienced deep rejection, abuse, or some combination of both in their lives, and as a result, they searched for acceptance in the only ways they knew how. The outcome was often devastating: abortion, affairs, jail time. You get the idea.

I love how God is using these women. I love to read and hear their stories of faith and redemption. I love to see them triumph in the face of deep woundedness. I'm amazed at how God does that. At the same time, my inner good girl pouts.

I am quietly angry.

I am a good girl with an unsensational story that will never make headlines or draw attention. The very thing I am passionate about, the very thing I am writing a book about, is the very thing I struggle with the most.

The reality of finding my significance in my performance is like putting lipstick and lace on a pig's dirty face.

I watch as my rebel counterparts tell dramatic stories of a lifetime of turning away. Then they have their come-to-Jesus moments, and I cheer them on, lift thankful hands, and wrap welcoming arms around them, the girls who made choices so different than my own.

Just yesterday I talked with the parent of a student in our church, who was lamenting over her prodigal daughter. At the end of our conversation, she said with great hope, "If she ever turns back to Jesus, she will have an *awesome* testimony." I know this mother is desperate for her daughter to walk with Jesus, to live in freedom, to know she is loved. And believing her daughter will one day have a beautiful testimony is perhaps this mother's way of holding on to hope. Still, the good girl in me wonders what those types of statements mean about those of us who never turned away in the first place. Does it mean our testimony is un-awesome? Does it mean maybe we don't have a testimony at all? Since when does the awesomeness of my testimony depend upon the extremity of my rebellion?

The good girl in me stands there with her arms crossed, wishing she had a story to tell that would draw crowds and change lives. In my mind, I know I'm better off without the scars and the hurt and the pain and the darkness. In my head, I know all the grace and love offered to them is available to me. But sometimes it doesn't feel fair that God seems to most powerfully use those who have chosen wrong and then come back again instead of those who did it right the first time. Where is the celebration for us?

So I retreat to my quiet room and open up my mask-wielding closet. In the safety of isolation, I take off that mask of good performance, hang it up for the night, and dare to ask the Lord why the rebels and the renegades get the parties. Why do the prodigal daughters get the glory? Where is my fattened calf?

I begin to question if I can ever experience the full measure of God's grace since my stories are so straight laced. Then, Shame chooses that moment to walk in and reintroduce herself, smiling as she sits on the corner of my bed with her *I told you so* and her sarcastic *You're not so good after all.*

I am forced to agree with her. I'm not so good after all.

I have issues. I still believe the crazy lie that God's acceptance of me is based on my performance. I'm still living in a small story that is all about me.

That is the raw of it, straight from my ugly. And I am left wondering what the Lord thinks about my mess. I don't have to wonder for long.

The Prodigal Question

One late night as I prepared for bed after a particularly difficult day, I was vaguely aware of the raw pull of mama guilt, monotone in the background like a leaky faucet—not an emergency unless you let it go too long.

In the midst of the guilt I didn't even know I was feeling concerning my responses to some of the events of the day, I had a fleeting thought of the story of the prodigal son. It was one of those moments with the Lord when I nearly turned my head to see if he was standing behind me. His voice was simple and direct: *How do you really feel about the prodigal son?*

Perhaps it was because the day had been hard and I was tired of keeping it together, but my answer was honest, immediate, abrupt, and embarrassing: *I'm mad.*

I have a reluctant kinship with the older brother in the Luke 15 story. The younger son asked for his share of his father's wealth and went off to a distant country to "squander his estate with loose living" (Luke 15:13). After that, there was a famine, and he was forced to find work by feeding pigs. He even began to crave pig food to sustain himself and was denied even that. He was in a bad way. When it got bad enough, he came to his senses and realized that even the servants in his father's house were treated better than this, so he decided to confess to his father and beg to be hired as a servant.

As it turns out, his father was waiting for him. While he was still a long way off, the father saw and had compassion on his son and ran to receive him. He dressed him in the best robe, put a ring on his hand and sandals on his feet. He called for a celebration, and that is what they had.

"Now his older son was in the field, and when he came and approached the house, he heard music and dancing" (Luke 15:25). The rebel had come home to a party. In the midst of the sound of happy celebration, the older son seethed outside and refused to go in.

As much as I want to be all rejoice-y and Jesus-y about the way the Father unconditionally accepts the prodigal back into the family, I am secretly and personally offended that this boy could be so irresponsible, thoughtless, immoral, and selfish and still be welcomed home. I'm mad that he went off and wasted money, caused heartache, had fun, and then was able to come home freely without question or judgment.

To find out what was going on, the older son summoned one of the servants. How interesting that it was more natural for him to get his information from a servant than to go directly to his father.

When the servant told him that his brother had come home and that his father killed the fattened calf and received him, the older son "became angry and was not willing to go in" (Luke 15:28). A son who knows he is accepted doesn't get angry and refuse to go in. Still, I stand up for that bitter older brother with discomforting passion.

Good girls think there should be consequences for the actions of the prodigal, not a party.

There should be a husband and a happy ending for the girl who has saved herself for marriage, not the one who was promiscuous ever since high school yet still landed the nice guy and just celebrated her fifth anniversary with a trip to Palm Springs.

There should be a baby for the couple who have faithfully prayed to get pregnant, not for the sixteen-year-old girl who had miserable sex one time with her boyfriend.

There should be reward for those who do good and pun-ishment for those who don't.

So we get angry. But good girls aren't supposed to be angry, so we convince ourselves we don't really care and it doesn't really matter. There's a party going on, but we refuse to go in. We hide behind this mask of indifference, pretending it doesn't bother us, because the only alternative is to face the source of the anger and what we are afraid to admit we believe: *How can he choose to reward them and ignore me?*

Reluctant Kinship

That night in my room, it was devastating for me to recognize my hardness of heart toward the wayward son. It was even more disturbing to admit how closely I identified with the older brother. I wanted to defend him, to stand up for him, to call all those around him to take notice of the work he had done, while his immoral, selfish, ungrateful brother went off and splurged until he had nothing left.

I knew I shouldn't be mad. I asked the Lord why he was bringing this up so randomly in the middle of my bedtime routine. No answer. I finally fell asleep. The next morning, it was still on my mind, my anger lingering like the misty fog on our front lawn. I picked up *Reflections for Ragamuffins* and turned to that day's date, half expecting what I would find. I am discovering the Lord to be gracious during my cur-rent life stage; he tends to get straight to the point with me, which I greatly appreciate. I shared a portion of this quote in chapter 7, but here it is in its entirety:

There is more power in sharing our weaknesses than our strengths. The forgiveness of God is gratuitous and uncon-ditional liberation from the domination of guilt. The sinful and repentant prodigal son experienced an intimacy and joy with his Father in his brokenness that his sinless self-righteous brother would never know.[1]

There it was again, a reference to the prodigal. And that familiar anger flared up a little. Why is it that the prodigal gets to experience intimacy and joy and the older son is left with nothing? I now knew the Lord wanted to show me something through this story, but I didn't know what. I began to take notice of how my connection to this story, this new kinship I had found with the older brother, played out in my daily life.

A few days later, I was in excellent spirits, even though the kids were sick with colds and we were unable to go to church. John went while we stayed home, played, decorated the Christmas tree, and were basically lazy. In a mixture of poor planning, miscommunication, and a bit of forgetfulness, I suddenly realized I had wasted a lot of time that morning and now the kids and I were not ready to go to meet family for lunch when we should have been. When John arrived home, he mentioned how I could have spent my time better that morning to prepare for our afternoon. At this, I was sent into a tailspin of self-hatred, shame, guilt, and anger. I was mad at myself. I needed to pay for my poor planning, my lack of good communication, and my forgetfulness.

When the day ended and I reflected upon how quickly I went from having a good day to wanting to cower in a dark corner of shame and regret, I once again remembered the story of the prodigal son.

When the older son stood outside the party, angry and wallowing in his own bitterness, the father came out, pleading with him to come in. The son refused to go in, *so the father came out*. And in the same way the father met the prodigal while he was still a long way off, the father met this older son while he stood outside the door. But while the prodigal received his father's love, the older son remained indifferent to it.

"But he answered and said to his father, 'Look! For so many years I have been serving you and I have never neglected

104

a command of yours; and yet you have never given me a young goat, so that I might celebrate with my friends; but when this son of yours came, who has devoured your wealth with prostitutes, you killed the fattened calf for him'" (Luke 15:29–30).

Notice the older son does not refer to the prodigal as "my brother" but as "this son of yours." He refuses to admit the relationship. He refuses to accept they are kin.

In that moment of feeling worthless, ashamed, and embarrassed at my lack of planning that afternoon, I discovered a new kinship, one that was foreign yet somehow familiar—one with the prodigal himself. It was then that I saw with new eyes how my lack of common ground with the prodigal son has kept me from experiencing the limitless, compassionate love of Christ. My unwillingness to admit my kinship with the prodigal, much like the older son, left me both right and lonely. It caused me not only to be unwilling to receive forgiveness from my heavenly Father, but unable to freely offer it, especially when it seemed it wasn't asked for or deserved.

My need for justice and my demand for payment have paralyzed me and oftentimes those in my family from living in freedom and joy. The power of sharing my weakness rather than living from my strength sounded both noble and impossible, not to mention terrifying.

A New Kinship

It was important for me to get to a place where I saw myself as a prodigal, because the weak recognize their need so much more quickly than the strong. The prodigal son didn't return the same way he left: proud, entitled, and immoral. He returned needy, repentant, and broken. The prodigal wasn't given a celebratory party while he was still proud and arrogant. He would not have been able to receive it yet. Rather, it wasn't until he came back in a posture of receptivity and humility. Still, if that's where it ends, there isn't much hope.

Jesus didn't die so I would feel a kinship with the prodigal, and he certainly didn't die so I could feel a kinship with the older brother.

That older son had a deep misunderstanding about his father's acceptance of him. He worked hard to try to get something he already had. He came in from the fields to the sound of music and dancing and lashed out at his father: "I serve you and you never had a party for me!"

But his father responds with compassion and truth. "Son, you have always been with me, and all that is mine is yours. But we had to celebrate and rejoice, for this brother of yours was dead and has begun to live, and was lost and has been found" (Luke 15:31–32).

All that is mine is yours. We already have the love and acceptance of our Father, so why do we try so hard to earn it? The older son missed out on the blessings and freedom to be found in his own home and chose to hide behind his anger instead. If the older brother would have gone in, he could have eaten and danced just like the others. If he had come to his father in the same way the prodigal had, he would have experienced the same love and acceptance every time. But he refused to go in.

The truth is, the prodigal son *was* wrong to squander his inheritance and to wear that mask of rebellion. The older brother was also wrong to be so angry and judgmental. What are these two things if not flesh patterns? Why would I want to identify with either one?

The beautiful, redemptive truth is, I am free to identify with the Father, the one who offered unconditional love and acceptance to both sons. I don't have to figure out the mess. I do have to trust in the One who can. He has always been with you, and all that is his is yours. Are you willing to step into the celebration and receive the gifts of your inheritance, or are you hanging around with the servants outside the doors?

 Behind the Mask

With whom do you most closely identify: the prodigal son or the older brother?

What are your honest, unedited thoughts about the father in this story?

In what ways are you living like a servant rather than a daughter?

Have you ever felt like your good girl life has left you with an unworthy testimony because you haven't experienced a period of rebellion? What makes a testimony worthy—the one rescued or the Rescuer?

10

·············

hide-and-seek

game over

One of the worst consequences of the Fall is the elaborate
barriers people erect between themselves and others.

—Sarah Young, *Jesus Calling*

We spend time each summer on Hilton Head Island
in South Carolina. Every year, I am surprised by
how hauntingly beautiful it is. The Spanish moss drapes lazy
over low branches, the moon hangs sweet over calm ocean
waters, the greenery is leafy and lush and full. I snap photos
in attempts to capture it, but I am never quite satisfied when
I see the images on the screen. There is a longing to take and
keep the beauty, a longing that is always disappointed.

We were made for paradise. We were made for the garden life. God has made everything beautiful in its time. "He
has also set eternity in the hearts of men; yet they cannot
fathom what God has done from beginning to end" (Eccles.
3:11 NIV).

From Beginning . . .

If the Garden of Eden were an ice cream sundae, then the man and the woman had all that and the cherry on top with a side of dreams come true. Their date nights were evening walks with the Creator of the universe. Exotic birds with shiny feathers and wings widespread sang them love songs. Her valentine gift was a field of untouched flowers and pure acceptance from the only man on earth. There was no competition, jealousy, or high expectations between them. Victoria had no secrets. All was laid bare and called holy, no need to hide. At least, not yet.

God was not merely the most important part of their relationship; he was the very air they breathed, exhibited days earlier when he breathed holy breath into the nostrils of the man he created from brown dirt. This fully human man and woman had spirits that were alive to God, just as it was meant to be. Their minds, wills, and emotions dwelled in the safety of their souls, untouched by doubt or fear or longing. God painted his love letters to them in sunset skies with wild, passionate strokes of brilliant orange and dazzling yellow. He wrapped acceptance around them like a warm breeze. They didn't have to wonder about the meaning of life. Life himself walked with them in the cool of the day.

> They were one and they were three: man, woman, and Creator.
> They were made in his image.
> They lacked nothing.
> Their needs were met.
> The Tree of Life stood tall and safe in the middle of the Garden.

But there was that other tree called Knowledge, the only one they weren't allowed to eat from. The only forbidden thing. He could have just made the good one so we wouldn't have a chance to wreck it all up. Love was not afraid to give us a choice even though he knew what would happen.

And so there were two trees, one representing a life dependent on God and the other representing a life dependent on self.

Enter the serpent, the crafty one, the liar.

He spoke to the woman from the branches of the self tree, challenging the word of God, offering an innocent question about God's seemingly unreasonable rule. "Indeed, has God said, 'You shall not eat from any tree of the garden'?" (Gen. 3:1).

He asks a question, intending to confuse and encourage doubt. The woman thinks, *No, not any tree. Just this one . . . right?* And she made her first mistake by entering into a conversation with the liar. Love was pushed aside. Need peeked its dormant head up from inside her fully accepted heart.

And then it got worse.

She tried to reason with him, telling him that God said they should not eat from or even touch the tree in the middle, or they would die. "From the fruit of the trees of the garden we may eat; but from the fruit of the tree which is in the middle of the garden, God has said, 'You shall not eat from it or touch it, or you will die'" (Gen. 3:2–3). She wanted to convince him, while secretly she was perhaps trying to convince herself of what she really believed.

And then the serpent told a blatant, blazing lie, the first lie recorded in the Bible. He spoke it out loud and on purpose, into the depths of her freshly troubled heart. "You surely will not die! For God knows that in the day you eat from it your eyes will be opened, and you will be like God, knowing good and evil" (Gen. 3:4–5).

Love dislodged itself from her heart, sending her spiraling down into despair and doubt and death. *Could it be true that God has more that he isn't giving? Could it be true that he is not who he says he is, who I thought he was, who I wish for him to be? Are my needs not really met?*

Doubt entered. She was dancing on dangerous garden grass, her soul in a battle with her God-united spirit. She began thinking things she'd never thought before and feeling things she'd never felt before.

I imagine in that moment she began to feel anxiety, uncertainty, suspicion, and anger for the first time in her existence. Perhaps God wasn't so good after all. He was holding out on them.

Satan lies. The woman doubts God in her soul, believes the lie of Satan, and chooses to take the fruit. In that moment, God's words come true, and though she continues standing there and is physically alive enough to hand the fruit to her husband, her spirit inside her dies, instantly and on the spot. Her God-united core is separated from him, as he cannot dwell where sin is.

A Good-Girl-Worthy Temptation

It's worth pointing out here that Satan didn't tempt Eve to act in a way that was outrageous. He didn't offer her riches or pornography or even a large piece of chocolate cake. It was fruit! Not even covered in caramel or anything. It didn't look so bad. If it had, perhaps she would not have been so easily deceived. What a perfect temptation for the good girl. The Bible says in Genesis 3:6 that "when the woman saw that the tree was good for food, and that it was a delight to the eyes . . . she took from its fruit and ate." Isn't that the type of thing good girls are tempted with, things that are pleasing to the eye? Like performing well but wanting the credit, or being strong all the time but having a hardened heart.

Eve took the fruit and gave some to her husband. He was with her, by the way. Did you imagine him all the way across the Garden, picking berries and sitting naked on a low tree branch? Genesis 3:6 says he was standing right there listening to the whole exchange, and he remained silent while he watched his wife be deceived.

Then he ate some, too.

111

Two Things

Satan did two things in the Garden that are vital to understand as we begin the process of letting go of our girl-made hiding places. First, he convinced Eve she had to *do* something in order to *be* something: If you eat the fruit, then you will be like God. Sound familiar?

If you serve in the church, then you will be acceptable.

If you are responsible, then you will be respected.

If you follow all the rules, then you will be good enough.

If you try hard, then you'll be more like God.

If you act righteous, then you will become righteous.

If you keep your house clean, then you will be a good wife.

If you make healthy dinners every night, then you will be a good mom.

If you wake up at 5 a.m. and pray every morning, then you will be a good Christian.

I'm certain you can think of some more do-to-be statements that you can personally identify with. Adam and Eve were tricked into believing they had to do something to get what they most longed for. To "be like God" is a shiny promise filled with great worth and holy significance.

The second thing that Satan did in the Garden is a little trickier, something many people go their whole lives without noticing. Something that makes the difference between living like a good girl and living in freedom. Something that is so important, so vital to our walk with God that I have to make a whole new paragraph for it just to make sure you don't miss it.

Satan told the woman, "You will be like God" (Gen. 3:5). But God had already covered that. In Genesis 1:27, God made man and woman in his own image. So what does that mean?

It means they already *were* like God, made in his likeness, bearing his image. Satan was promising something to them that God had already graciously and lovingly provided. Satan convinced them to forget God's gift and try to work for it instead.

112

I liken that to someone saying something like this to my twin daughters: "Hey girls! Go to the store and buy matching outfits. Then put them on, dance around, and you'll be twins." The truth is, they were born twins. Whether they dress alike or if one dresses like a clown while the other one is naked, the fact remains that they are twins. They were conceived at the same time to the same parents, and they were born three minutes apart. It doesn't matter if they grow up and get in a fight, move hundreds of miles apart, and refuse to admit the existence of the other. They are still twins.

Birth determines identity.

Adam and Eve were birthed, or created, in the image of God. Period.

But they didn't remember. Not only that, the gift was subtly twisted, and the holy, image-bearing truth of Genesis 1:27 was no longer enough. They didn't just want to be like God, bearing his image. They wanted to *be* God, self-sufficient and independent.

As a result, every human after that is born separated from God, born of Adam and Eve, born into a sin identity. The human condition is such that birth determines identity—so now humankind is birthed into Adam. "For the sin of this one man, Adam, caused death to rule over many" (Rom. 5:17 NLT).

The only thing Satan could promise them was something they already had. Because Satan had nothing new to give them that wasn't already theirs. The only power he had was the power of the lie. If he could trick them into forgetting that they were made in God's image, then he could get them to do crazy things, which is exactly what happened.

The First Hiding

As soon as Adam and Eve made the choice to believe Satan and forget God, they did the only thing that felt right at the time: they hid. The first mask was made out of fig leaves sewn together in fear and chaos with trembling hands and a mounting sense of urgency. Dudley Hall says it this way: "All of fallen humanity has a consciousness of being incomplete and flawed. This is the result of original sin in the human race. We are imperfect in the presence of God who is absolutely perfect. So we stand vulnerable to exposure but terribly afraid. How do we handle it? We do what Adam and Eve did; we dive behind a bush—scrambling for something that will cover our sense of unworthiness and shame."[1]

"When the cool evening breezes were blowing, the man and his wife heard the LORD God walking about in the garden. So they hid from the LORD God among the trees. Then the LORD God called to them, 'Where are you?'" (Gen. 3:8–9 NLT). He walked and he searched, but he already knew. The man and the woman chose to believe the lie of Satan rather than trust in the word of God. They chose to sin, to depend on something other than God to get their needs met.

The good girl in me says they got what they deserved. Disobedience demands punishment. I cry out for justice and judgment, as if I would have behaved differently given the chance. Yet, another part of me recognizes myself in the man and the woman. I am given the chance to believe God on a daily basis and I continue to forget what I long to remember. Those who do not know God have only death to choose. Those who do know him have a choice, but they don't know it.

We hide, too. I hide behind my mask of performance so people will think I am smart, capable, and put together. I hide behind the reputation I have established rather than risk trusting an unpredictable Jesus. I hide behind my positive emotions rather than let you see my reality. I hide behind my list of rules so I can check off each one, as if I'm another step closer to God because I've followed them. I hide behind my mask of strength because I'm ashamed of my weakness.

Where are you? God asks, not because he doesn't know, but because he knows I have to come out of hiding in order to be found. To be healed. To be whole.

Here is the thing about the mask: there is nothing good about it. It can't be fixed, polished, or taught to behave differently. God has another word for the masks we wear to get our needs met. In fact, he talks about these masks in great detail. The Bible calls the masks we depend on *flesh* and consistently contrasts this with the Spirit.

> For those who are according to the flesh set their minds on the things of the flesh, but those who are according to the Spirit, the things of the Spirit. (Rom. 8:5)

> It is the Spirit who gives life; the flesh profits nothing; the words that I have spoken to you are spirit and are life. (John 6:63)

> For the flesh sets its desire against the Spirit, and the Spirit against the flesh; for these are in opposition to one another, so that you may not do the things that you please. (Gal. 5:17)

The Spirit and the flesh are in opposition. It doesn't matter if your flesh looks bad or good; it opposes the Spirit within you, and this struggle can rob us from living out of our true, Jesus-made identity. Knowing this begs the question: How could this good girl possibly expect to please God by depending on her masks, or her flesh, if the flesh opposes the Spirit of God?

The First Finding

Back in the Garden, the guilty couple's response was exactly as it should have been. They sinned against God, and they were guilty. But if all they felt was guilt, they would have run at top speed back to the arms of their Father. But guilt wasn't their only problem. They felt shame on top of guilt, and so they crafted a mask for themselves, a hiding place where they thought they wouldn't be found. They needed more than a place to hide; they needed forgiveness and they needed life. God lovingly, graciously, and miraculously provided both.

115

God did not let the man and the woman remain hidden behind the masks they fashioned for themselves. They were aware of their need, but their dark world was now hanging upside down. They didn't know which way was up.

And so, God killed an innocent animal right there in the Garden, the first sacrifice for sin that pointed to the future sacrifice of Christ. Because of his great love and compassion, God provided an escape for humankind by holding back the wrath they actually deserved. We call this mercy.

But simply providing escape isn't enough. Mercy, as beautiful as it is, is only protection. And so God made garments of skin for them from the sacrificed animal. In doing so, he gave them something they did not deserve. We call this grace. He took away the hiding place they crafted for themselves and made for them a new one on his terms.

Mercy protects. Grace provides.

And a few thousand years later, he would send the Second Adam, one who lived a full human life and ate only from the Tree of Life, depending entirely on his Father in ways the first Adam failed to do. "For the sin of this one man, Adam, caused death to rule over many. But even greater is God's wonderful grace and his gift of righteousness, for all who receive it will live in triumph over sin and death through this one man, Jesus Christ" (Rom. 5:17 NLT). In the person of Jesus, mercy and grace show up perfect and pour out all over us.

Paul says it again in 1 Corinthians 15:21–22: "For since by a man came death, by a man also came the resurrection of the dead. For as in Adam all die, so also in Christ all will be made alive." God knew they needed a hiding place, but he did not let them stay in hiding on their own terms. And he doesn't let us, either.

The Hiding Place of Shame

God takes any kind of sin very seriously; so seriously, in fact, that he would never dream of expecting us to handle it on our own. It's too big, too bad, too much. So he sent the law to let unbelievers know how bad it is, he sent his Son to pay for it, and he sent his Spirit to give us the authority to resist it. When we sin, guilt is the right response. Guilt is used by God to show us our need for him. Guilt is not our problem. If all we felt were guilt, we would admit the wrong and run to God for help. But that is not what we do.

We feel guilt for not measuring up, but then we feel shame on top of that. And shame is a different thing altogether.

Guilt says I did wrong.
Shame says I am wrong.
Guilt deals with behavior.
Shame deals with identity.
Guilt leads to repentance.
Shame leads to hiding.

I couldn't sleep the other night because I was thinking of all the ways I should be doing life better. My good-girl checklist was full of to-dos and not one of them was checked off.

Shame rolls 'round and 'round my heart and head every day of my life. I would rather call it guilt because it doesn't sound as embarrassing, but really I think it goes deeper. Guilt is a good thing, a God-reminder when things aren't right and an opportunity to change them. Shame is what happens when we let guilt fester and sink deeper and don't deal with it. Shame seeps into our skin when we aren't looking and takes our spirit hostage. And then she sits down heavy and masks herself as us so we can't tell the difference between the two.

Shame waits until my defenses are down on a sleepless night and then begins to whisper doubt: *Maybe you're not doing enough. Maybe you're not cut out for this. Maybe you're messing them up. Who do you think you are?*

And in that place, I have a choice. I can believe the dark suggestions that it is up to me to get it right on my own. Or

I can trust that I was made in God's image for such a time as this, to parent these children he has given and to receive grace and mercy from his hand.

As believers in Jesus, as receivers of the gift of his death and his life, both our guilt problem and our shame problem have been dealt with. But just like the pitiful couple in the Garden, we don't know it. We still feel guilty when we sin, as we should. Yet, instead of taking our inabilities, weaknesses, and shortcomings to God, we choose to try to deal with sin ourselves and hide behind try-hard masks. I look to myself as my only point of reference.

Here's the truth: aside from accepting Jesus as your personal Savior, there is nothing left to do to gain God's favor. Nothing. And that means no thing.

The Hiding Place of Grace

When God killed an innocent animal in the Garden, he showed mercy to Adam and Eve, holding back the wrath they deserved. He did the same thing for us by sending the innocent Christ, showing mercy by punishing him with the punishment meant for us. We know about this one. We sing about this one. Jesus died on the cross.

In their book *The Rest of the Gospel*, Dan Stone and Greg Smith talk about what they call the Doublecross, or the fact that the cross of Christ is two-sided. The first side is the blood side where Christ died for us, offering forgiveness. This was represented in the Garden with the killing of the animal.

But there is a second side to the cross. This one is more difficult, more intangible, and frankly, less believable. In the Garden, God not only displayed his mercy by holding back the wrath the man and woman deserved; he also showed them grace by clothing them with garments from that animal, giving them something they *didn't deserve*. And so the second side of the cross is the body side, offering life.[2]

We celebrate it once a year on Easter, where we remember how Christ's physical body died, was buried, and rose up again. We also celebrate it at the communion table, where we drink the cup (representing his blood) and eat the bread (representing his body). But other than those two remembrances, the resurrected Christ doesn't get much airtime in our minds. The first side is where most good girls live. We know about the forgiveness, about the sin and the blood and the death of Christ. But we aren't as familiar with the body side. So we live on the forgiveness side and try hard to get the life.

It is true that Christ died for us. But it is also true that *we died with him*. And if we died with him, then when he was buried, we were buried. And when he rose up from the dead, we rose up from the dead. It sounds crazy. But the Bible says it's true:

> Therefore we have been buried with Him through baptism into death, so that as Christ was raised from the dead through the glory of the Father, so we too might walk in newness of life. For if we have become united with Him in the likeness of His death, certainly we shall also be in the likeness of His resurrection, knowing this, that our old self was crucified with Him, in order that our body of sin might be done away with, so that we would no longer be slaves to sin; for he who has died is freed from sin. Now if we have died with Christ, we believe that we shall also live with Him. (Rom. 6:4–8)

So what difference does this co-death, co-burial, and co-resurrection make in our daily lives? Every difference. Now, we do not have to manufacture our own safe places.

We have been placed into safety.

"For you have died and your life is hidden with Christ in God" (Col. 3:3). This is a different kind of hiding than the one we have practiced as good girls. When we realize the safe place where we dwell, there is new hope for the entire human race to breathe a collective sigh of sweet relief. God has provided a better way and because of that, there is a new way to live.

God, who is love, loves you. Now, you can love others by serving as he leads. God says you already measure up in Christ (2 Cor. 3:5–6). All your needs are met in Christ (Phil. 4:19). Now, you can listen and respond to his voice. In Christ, your spirit is united with God's Spirit so it is possible to avoid sin (Col. 3:5–11). You are righteous because of Christ (2 Cor. 5:21). Now you are free to live like it's true.

In the try-hard life, your behavior determines your identity. But these verses describe a person who is loved by God with no strings attached. This new way of life is only possible because of Christ, not because of anything we have done. I believe the good girl longs to live from this new place. Still, knowing the truth is one thing; experiencing it is entirely another.

Learning from a River

My husband and I dated for nearly two years before we were married. Most of those years were spent apart. He was in seminary while I was finishing college in a different state, so a lot of our communication was based on phone calls and email. One summer while he was living in Atlanta, he sent me an email that forever changed how I think about life with God. He was struggling through a period of doubt and worry. This is a portion of what he said, minus the mushy stuff:

Subject: the living God
Date: Wed, 9 Aug 2000
The Lord spoke to my heart last night in the midst of all the feelings and thoughts I've been having. It was as if He said, *Experience the living God.* I didn't really know what that meant outside of the simple message, but was certain that the words were spoken quietly to my heart.

Today, I went on a two-mile hike in the woods to the Chattahoochee River. I wanted to get some exercise and spend time with God on the river. I didn't know what this particular river looked like, so I wasn't sure what I was looking for. As I hiked, I kept repeating this phrase and asking God about it: *Experience the living God.*

I found my way down to a dumpy, stagnant river, maybe ten feet wide and barely running. *The Chattahoochee River*, I thought to myself. *Some river.* I snapped a picture and prepared to leave . . . until I heard something in the distance and noticed an opening in the trees. I walked through the woods and there it was—the Chattahoochee River. I was eye-level to the most enormous river I had ever seen rushing powerfully in one direction. As soon as I saw it, there was a whisper in my soul: *Experience the living God.*

I picture him standing there on the bank of that awe-inspiring river, listening to the voice of his Father speak truth into his heart while the roar of the river was loud and fresh in his ears. This river was like the *living God*, a picture of a life hidden with Christ. That other stagnant stream was like the good girl's efforts to live, love, and serve out of her own resources. She would be crazy to return to the fake Chattahoochee after seeing the beauty of the authentic one. Why would anyone do that?

God's desire is that we live in freedom and drink from the wide, deep, powerful River of Life. The masks we hide behind keep us from experiencing the fullness of life the way we were meant to live it. Do you dare believe it is safe to take them off and live like Jesus is a real God-man who really was and really is and really makes a difference?

Behind the Mask

Can you think of any more "do-to-be" statements you have lived by in your own life? Do any of those contradict what Scripture says has already been done?

We have talked about the two trees in the Garden of Eden—
the Tree of Life and the Tree of the Knowledge of Good
and Evil. Have you ever considered the fact that the
forbidden tree was not just offering the knowledge of
evil, but the knowledge of good as well? Why would
God want to protect us from the knowledge of good?

Read Galatians 5:17 again. "For the flesh sets its desire
against the Spirit, and the Spirit against the flesh; for
these are in opposition to one another, so that you may
not do the things that you please." If our mask repre-
sents our flesh, then is it possible to ever please God by
living from behind it?

....

the finding

*Y*ou have caught a glimpse of the God Who Sees. You know there is more to him than you once thought. And you know there is more to you. You want to come out, to let yourself be found by Love, to release your tight hold on familiar. The false hiding place beckons you back to the dark with loud whispers of warning: *It isn't safe! Don't go out there!* But you know there has been a rescue. "For He rescued us from the domain of darkness, and transferred us to the kingdom of His beloved Son" (Col. 1:13).

Darkness is the only choice for the girl who doesn't believe. But we have been rescued from that darkness. We have been picked up and placed into light. So why do we still try to live as though we haven't? God has drawn us to himself, like a Daddy who scoops up his girl into loving, strong arms and pulls her close, warm and safe.

But good girls who hide have to experience two rescues, much like the two-sided cross in the previous chapter. The good girl understands the basic foundation of her salvation: forgiveness of sin. That first rescue happens at salvation, the initial transfer from darkness to light. In that moment, her life is hidden with Christ in God (see Col. 3:3). The rescue is actually, factually

123

complete. *But the good girl doesn't know about this hiding with Christ.* She does not understand the depth and breadth and height and width of this Lover who came for her, and so this rescue seems inadequate. She lives on the forgiveness side of the cross and then begins to work to earn the life.

Her genuine thankfulness toward the Rescuer at first looks like gratitude, and indeed it is. But when she begins to realize how hard it is to measure up, she grows resentful and the gratitude morphs into duty. She compares herself to rescued others and feels both less-than and better-than, proud and invisible. To cover her lack, she puts up a mask and crafts a new dark place.

She has already been transferred into the light, but she is hiding under the covers. And so she needs a new rescue. This time, she needs to be rescued from *herself.* And how she longs to be found.

I understood at an early age about the first rescue. Jesus came to save sinners. He came for the lost, the broken, the hurt, and the lonely. He came to heal sick people and to raise dead people and to die for the sins of everyone.

Never once did I consider he also came to save me from myself. I'm a good girl who has done good things and has good intentions for the world around me. What harm could I do to myself? But then I reconsider, and I think of the effort and the work. And then the shame. I think of the worry that keeps me up at night and the fear that perhaps I've not done enough. I think of the way I compare myself and the pain that comes when I grasp for worth and security from my husband or my job or my children.

Jesus came to save me from myself. He came to save me from self-effort. He didn't just die for my sin to give me forgiveness; he rose again to give me life. And so he beckons me, "*Come.*"

Arise, my darling, my beautiful one, and come with me. See! The winter is past; the rains are over and gone. Flowers appear on the earth; the season of singing has come, the cooing of doves is heard in our land. The fig tree forms its early fruit; the blossoming vines spread their fragrance. Arise, come, my darling; my beautiful one, come with me. (Song of Sol. 2:10–13 NIV)

When I first began to see the depravity of my masks, I was overwhelmed, overcome, and undone. I felt hopeless to ever change, to ever be different. I sat across from a trusted friend and counselor in Brentwood, Tennessee, during the summer of 2000. Slumped over in a worn-out chair, I confessed, "I don't know how *not* to be this way." This coping, these masks, this life motivated by fear was all I knew. I was waiting for him to unveil a five-, ten-, or hundred-step program to teach me what to do and how to live, real and free. I would do anything.

A small smile played its way across his face, and what he said next was the most freeing, simple, and life-changing thing that has yet been said to me. "You're *not* this way. This may be how you cope, but this is not who you are."

It might look different for you, the way you move from one hiding to the other, from mask wearing to Jesus rest. But Colossians 3 so beautifully outlines what it has looked like for me:

Receive "Let the peace of Christ rule in your hearts." (v. 15)

Remain "Let the word of Christ richly dwell within you." (v. 16)

Respond "Whatever you do in word or deed, do all in the name of the Lord Jesus, giving thanks through Him to God the Father." (v. 17)

Remember "Set your mind on the things above, not on the things that are on earth. For you have died and your life is hidden with Christ in God." (vv. 2–3)

Yes, they all begin with *re-*. But please don't let that fool you into thinking this is some kind of formula. This recovering good girl has lived too long chasing formulas and how-tos.

Michelangelo didn't teach people how to paint. He painted. Pavarotti didn't become one of the most commercially successful tenors of all time by talking about how to sing. He sang. Would you rather listen to Michael Jordan talk about how to play basketball or have a front row seat at a game? The originator of all art and talent and beauty and love lives in us. Why do we insist upon pinning him down to a list?

I can't tell you how to walk with Jesus, but I can share my stories. The flat, bullet-point, how-to Jesus I feebly worshiped while hiding behind my masks is an imposter. The real, alive, redeemer Jesus longs to take his place in our lives. But first we have to receive him. Not just for salvation, but for *life*.

11

on truth and trusting

receive

on truth and trusting

Let the peace of Christ rule in your hearts, to which indeed
you were called in one body; and be thankful.
—Colossians 3:15

My favorite movie as a girl was *The Wizard of Oz.*
I thought Judy Garland as Dorothy was the most
beautiful girl I had ever seen. I idolized Dorothy. She was
innocent, loving, and kind. That voice, that dress, that dog,
those shoes! She had it all. Years later when I heard her described as chubby in movie commentaries, I was so confused.
Chubby? Hardly. To me, she was perfect.

I've seen the movie countless times, to the point where I
not only know nearly every line, I also know hand movements
and head tilts. I own the collector's edition hardcover copy of
the script. I can sing the scene in Munchkin Land from the

coroner to the Lollipop Guild. I know how to spot nearly all of the many goofs and bloopers, like how Dorothy's dark, swiss-cake-roll pigtails change length from scene to scene and how props reappear in the wrong places.

In the '80s, one of the networks always aired *The Wizard of Oz* on a Friday night in the fall. So every Saturday toward the end of the summer, I would find the TV Guide section of the newspaper and check the listings for the next Friday night. We had no VCR, no Blockbuster, no Hulu, no Netflix. If I missed it, that was it for a whole year.

Missing it was not an option.

I remember the night before the movie came on, my knees would ache and I couldn't sleep for all the excitement. I loved the music, especially the quick, high-pitched chorus that played when the sojourning foursome first glimpsed the Emerald City right after the snow wakes them up in the poppy field: "*You're out of the woods, you're out of the dark, you're out of the night! Step into the sun, step into the light!*"

I've thought about this movie a lot as I have grown up. The Scarecrow wanted a brain; the Tin Man, a heart. The Lion longed for courage, and all Dorothy wanted was to find a way home. They followed yellow brick roads, ran from flying monkeys, and even risked their lives to get the Wicked Witch's broomstick just like the Wizard—who really was no Wizard at all—told them to. They did it all because they longed for something they did not have. In the end, though, we learn that they had it all along; they just didn't know it. They worked, they chased, they strived, and they feared, all in an effort to get what they already had.

After all, the Scarecrow was often the one to devise the plans; the Tin Man rusted from crying real, heartfelt tears; and the Lion found the courage to save Dorothy, all before they received anything from the Wizard. Dorothy was the most obvious of all. She couldn't take a step without being aware of those sparkly, ruby slippers. Still, when she finally sees Glinda, she cries out for help and is told she's always had the power to go back to Kansas. The slippers she wore all along were the very means by which she would make her way home.

But she didn't know it.

Knowing what you have makes all the difference. As believers, we have been given everything we need for life and godliness, but if we don't know it, we will never experience the reality of it.

As we talk more about what we have been given in Christ and about moving from hiding behind our masks to a life hidden with Christ in God, it is important to keep Colossians 3:3 in mind: "For you have died and your life is hidden with Christ in God." The question that immediately comes to my mind is this: *I'm not dead, I'm alive. So what died?* To understand the answer, it is vital to discover what the Bible says about our invisible insides.

Soul vs. Spirit

In everyday conversation, we often use the words *soul* and *spirit* interchangeably. For the sake of communicating trivial stuff, it's a fairly harmless assumption. But when it comes to understanding how to come out from behind the masks we wear and live in freedom from those false identities, the distinction between soul and spirit becomes a vital part of our experience. This biblical distinction is often overlooked.

> Now may the God of peace Himself sanctify you entirely; and may your spirit and soul and body be preserved complete, without blame at the coming of our Lord Jesus Christ. (1 Thess. 5:23)

We are a three-part whole, a spirit being with a soul who lives in a body. For me, understanding this difference is key to experiencing the abundant life available to us in Christ.

The Visible Invisible

Most people would at least admit that humans are a two-part whole: one part seen, the other part unseen. Our bodies are a dwelling place, a vessel made to carry our invisible around. I attended several funerals as a kid, and all of them had open caskets. I remember staring at my grandfather's chest, willing it to move. There was a moment when I was sure I saw the rise and fall of it, ever so slight. My eyes were not accustomed to seeing a person without their invisible. His body was there, but *he* was not. So what was missing? The invisible can be overlooked until it isn't there anymore.

Though most people would admit that there is a visible and an invisible, there is some debate as to what our invisible is made up of. Teachers, preachers, and theologians have many differing views on what the Bible teaches on this. Personally, I'm convinced that the Bible teaches that we are a three-part whole, and that God's Word is the only thing that can separate the two invisibles from one another. "For the word of God is living and active and sharper than any two-edged sword, and piercing as far as the division of soul and spirit, of both joints and marrow, and able to judge the thoughts and intentions of the heart" (Heb. 4:12).

What does the difference matter? So we have both a soul and a spirit. Big deal. It's invisible, so what difference does it make? I am not an anatomy expert by any measure, but I think understanding the physical aspects of joints and marrow could provide insight into the difference between soul and spirit.

The Anatomy of the Visible

A joint is the point where two bones in the body connect. Joints form three categories of movability: freely movable, slightly movable, and immovable.

Freely movable joints are those that provide the greatest range of motion, like elbows, knees, shoulders, and hips. The second type of joint is *slightly movable,* like the individual vertebrae in our spine. Based on what those major joints are doing (running, jumping, walking), the slightly movable joints will react accordingly. So the vertebrae in our back respond to the actions of our bodies, though their movement is limited.

The third type of joint is *immovable,* or fixed. Fibers of connective tissue in the skull make up one kind of immovable joint, while the other is that of teeth sitting still in their sockets.

Likewise, there are two types of bone marrow: yellow and red. When the body goes into starvation mode, it draws upon the fat stored in the yellow marrow in order to get energy. The red marrow is made up of red blood cells, platelets, and white blood cells that travel to the blood to do important jobs. They carry oxygen and nutrients to other parts of the body and fight disease and infection.[1]

Both joints and marrow are vital parts of our bodies. But without the marrow, the joints are useless. Bone marrow is the life-giving substance without which we would cease to exist. Joints are only useful for a person if their body is alive.

The Anatomy of the Invisible

Like the joints in our bodies, the soul is also made up of three categories of movability: the emotions, the mind, and the will.

When I think about those freely movable joints, I think about my feelings. The phrase "knee-jerk reaction" comes to mind, referring to the reaction of someone who didn't have time to think through a response. Instead, they simply acted on their feelings. The freely movable joints are like the emotional part of the soul. Changeable. Reactionary. Obvious.

The second category, the slightly movable part of the soul, is the mind. Our minds only go one of two ways: truth or lies. Much like the vertebrae that simply react to the movement of those bigger joints, our minds are often swayed by what our feelings tell us. So if I feel rejected, I'm likely to believe that

131

I am unacceptable. If I feel embarassed, I'm likely to believe that I am a fool. If I feel capable, I'm likely to believe I can handle anything.

The third, fixed part of the soul is the will of the chooser. This is where we are moved to action. Our will takes into consideration what our mind and emotions are telling us, and then we decide how we are going to respond.

Stopping here is bad news for the good girl because it means that my experience in life is dependent upon what I feel and think. There is no alternative to my own point of view. I am held captive by my own thoughts and emotions. I am my only point of reference. This is a picture of someone who doesn't know God.

In the same way that the joints in our body can't function properly without the life-giving marrow, our soul can't function properly without the life-giving spirit. Because of the fall of man, as we talked about in chapter 10, we are all born separated from God. Clearly, an unbeliever has a body (the ability to run, walk, see, smell, taste, and hear) and a soul (the ability to think, feel, and choose). But apart from God, *their spirit is dead*. There is no ability to commune with God. They can't work it, trick it, or force it alive.

Back in the Garden, when God said that eating from the Tree of Knowledge would lead to death, he was not saying that just to scare the man and woman. Did they die physically? No, they still had bodies. Did their souls die? No, they still had emotions and thoughts and wills of their own. So what died?

Their spirits died that day in the Garden, that invisible place deep inside where they were connected to their God. And so every human after that was born into Adam, into death, with a dead spirit.

The only way to bring the spirit to life is to admit it is dead and receive the One who is Life. When my spirit meets God's Holy Spirit, life is made available. Now I have a choice. I can either receive truth from my circumstances by responding to what my soul tells me, or I can believe that God's Spirit is now united with my spirit and receive truth from him.

The Letting

Knowing the truth is essential. Dorothy walked all over Oz and Munchkin Land in those ruby slippers without knowing they were her ticket home. At the end of the movie when Glinda finally told her she always had the power to go back to Kansas, she knew the truth. But simply knowing it wasn't enough. Once she knew it, she had to *let it be true*. As the song says, she had to "march up to the gate *and bid it open*." There is a lot to the letting. I make it harder than it needs to be.

We have the letting power.

If I cling to my *if-I-could-onlys* and my *if-they-would-justs*, I miss out on the freedom to be found in letting peace rule. The truth is true whether I let it be or not. Colossians says to *let the peace of Christ rule in your hearts*.

When I hear the word *peace*, I tend to think of woven crowns of dandelions on top of the unbrushed hair of barefooted hippies. I think of cliché beauty pageant answers and Richard Nixon standing at the top of airplane steps. The word *rule* in this verse is the Greek word *brabeuō*, which literally means "to act as umpire."[2]

> um·pire: one having authority to decide finally a controversy or question between parties: as **a** : one appointed to decide between arbitrators who have disagreed[3]

There is indeed a controversy between two parties: my flesh and my spirit, the lies and the truth, the fake and the real, the mask and the Savior. Peace stands between them, looks me straight in the eye, and asks permission to do what peace does best: give rest. God offers his peace to act as my umpire, to release me from having to be the authority and keep it together. But I have to let peace be peaceful within

133

me. I have to receive this peace. It is not an easy thing to do, to quiet the voices of the accusing party and to allow peace to have the authority. If I will let it, the peace of Christ will stand between me and the lies of my enemy, the lies that accuse and attack and shame. Letting this peace rule is a profound mystery, and for many years, it seemed impossible.

The Mystery

As a good girl, I lived a lot of my life believing that other people knew a secret about being a believer that I wasn't privy to. So I strived and tried and worked hard to find it. And when I couldn't figure it out, I wore all my masks to cover up what I thought I lacked. If I couldn't feel complete, I could at least look like I was. My masks bought me time while I figured out what the secret was.

There isn't exactly a secret, but there is a mystery to this Christ-life: now you have a choice. Before you knew Christ, you had no choice but to live from the mask. Born as a daughter of Eve, your flesh was your only option because your spirit was dead.

But now that you believe, now that you have been reborn in your invisible self, now that God's Spirit has given birth to your spirit, now you have a choice: live from your flesh, your false identity, your mask. Or live from your spirit, your true identity, and your freedom. You have the letting power. Let fear dominate or let peace rule.

The mystery has now been made known.

All of life comes down to this choice. Once you discover the mystery, once you experience the living God, there is no going back to the fake Chattahoochee. Paul describes it as "the mystery which has been hidden from the past ages and generations, but has now been manifested to His saints, to whom God willed to make known what is the riches of the glory of this mystery among the Gentiles, *which is Christ in you, the hope of glory*" (Col. 1:26–27, emphasis added).

134

There is no other hope but the truth of Christ in you. There are those who will say that obedience is the key to the Christian life, and that to say otherwise is to wave the dangerous, offensive flag of passivity over our churches. To that, I will simply say this: good girls live obediently, but they do not know the mystery. They obey from their mask, from their fear, from their flesh on the soul level. They are obedient to the law. Jesus calls us to a new and better way. He still asks for our obedience, but it is no longer obedience to the law. Now we are called as believers to be obedient to the truth.

Paul writes to the church of Galatia, "You were running a good race. Who cut in on you and kept you from obeying the truth?" (Gal. 5:7 NIV). This obedience to the truth doesn't come naturally or automatically. There is laboring. There is striving. But this striving labor has the potential to be new and light and joyful.

"We proclaim Him, admonishing every man and teaching every man with all wisdom, so that we may present every man complete in Christ. For this purpose also I labor, *striving according to His power, which mightily works within me*" (Col. 1:28–29, emphasis added). The work is not according to the mask we wear; it is according to his power that works within us. It isn't an external attempt to live up to the law; it occurs on the spirit level where we are united with Christ. What does that look like? Paul isn't done yet. "Therefore as you have received Christ Jesus the Lord, so walk in Him, having been firmly rooted and now being built up in Him and established in your faith, just as you were instructed, and overflowing with gratitude" (Col. 2:6–7).

How did you receive him? By faith. We tell unbelievers there is nothing they can do to be saved except to receive that which Christ has done. And then when they receive him and discover struggle and hardship on the other side, we tell them to keep on trying to do what Jesus would do. In other words, you may have been saved by faith, but now it's time to try really hard to make life work. That is not what the Bible says, yet that is what we live. We are to walk with him in the same way we received him: *by faith*.

Release

Perhaps you've heard or said statements like these: "I just want to become more like Jesus," or, "I should do what Jesus would do in this situation." These statements are heavy with the implication that Jesus is way out there in front of me on the proverbial path of life, and I am going to have to somehow gather my wits to decide to catch up to him. It feels both impossible and overwhelming. The good girl in me wants to try, but the shamed girl in me wants to give up.

There *is* a becoming that happens as we walk with Jesus, but it isn't under a system of achieving. Rather, it is in the act of receiving. In order to receive, we have to first let go, to honestly release our right to hold on to those things we trust in for life, those counterfeit sources of truth and security, those false hiding places that seem to offer peace but leave us feeling restless.

It is so hard to let go of the mask because we sincerely believe we'll be left with nothing. So even though I loathe the pain, the fear, and the worry, at least they are mine. Familiar. Comfortable. *Mine.* We coddle and protect our right to hold on to the things we have learned to trust in and dare God to try to remove them. We feel safe-ish in our hiding place and we fear exposure more than we long for freedom.

These faces I wear are not masks, you say. *They are me. This is me. This is who I am.* The only problem with owning this masked identity is that Jesus has nothing to do with it. It's all about me and my good intentions and my effort to be something. Since when does the creation get to decide its own use? Does not the Creator determine the worth and identity of his craftsmanship? Does not the God of the Universe have the final word on the belovedness of his own? If you want to embrace the reality of who he is and who he has made you to be, you first have to release the lie of who you always thought you were.

You are not accepted because you are good.
You are free to be good because you are accepted.
You are not responsible to have it all together.
You are free to respond to the One who holds all things in his hands.
You do not have to live up to impossible expectations.
You are free to wait expectantly on Jesus, the One who is both author and perfecter of your faith.

Receive

We have a God who knows what it is to sacrifice. Christ became weak and vulnerable, releasing his right to be strong. He was exposed, releasing his right to hide. He was disrespected, releasing his right to a good reputation. He forgave, releasing the right to take offense. He was rejected, humbled, and emptied. He gave up his life in order to give it to you.

When you let go of those things you have let define you all your life, you will not be left with nothing. The story of redemption and healing is that Jesus came to exchange my not-good-enough with his better-than-I-could-ever-imagine. He came to trade my life for his, my weak for his strong, my ashes for his beauty. He longs for us to receive the gift of himself.

In a little book called *Let God Love You*, author and speaker Malcolm Smith encourages performers and achievers to receive the love of God wholly and completely. "When we try to earn His love or be worthy of it, we actually push ourselves away from it. Because His love arises from who He is, it must always be a gift, always freely bestowed upon us, always unconditional. Why does the sun shine on the lake? . . . The sun shines on the lake because the lake is there! The lake is warm and radiant, shining like the sun because the sun first shone on it."[4]

God longs for us to receive our present God-given, Jesus-purchased, Holy Spirit–empowered identity. He does not ask us to chase witches or escape flying monkeys or deliver broomsticks. He asks us to open our hands, receive the gift, and then live as if it were true. Are you trying to be who Jesus wants you to be? Or do you trust him to bring out who he has already created you to be? It is vital to recognize the difference between these two questions because one leads to death, the other leads to life.

I spent many years trying to be who I thought Jesus wanted me to be. I used the fruit of the Spirit as the ultimate good-girl checklist. My senior year in high school, I began each week by writing a different fruit of the Spirit in my planner with the intention of working on that particular characteristic that week. *JOY. This week, I will work hard to be joyful.* By lunch on Monday, I was done. Failed. The Christian life was officially impossible. Rather than admitting I couldn't measure up to the standard God had set, I thought I wasn't trying hard enough. Just like Adam and Eve in the Garden, who hid when they sinned, I refused to face my loving Father with my own lack and wallowed in shame instead. *If I could just be more like Jesus. What is wrong with me?*

I had an inaccurate idea of the fruit of the Spirit. Rather than a checklist of things we are to work on, the Galatians 5:22–23 list is a beautiful description of a Person who lives in us: "But the fruit of the Spirit is love, joy, peace, patience, kindness, goodness, faithfulness, gentleness, self-control." The Greek word translated "goodness" (*agathōsynē*) means inherently good.

But wait! you say. *I thought this isn't about our performance!* It isn't. This is a list of the fruit of the Spirit, not the fruit of the flesh. The goodness Paul talks about here does not come from our mask, or our flesh. This good is a result of the Spirit within us. Goodness is a fruit or a natural outcome, not a try-hard workout. Only Jesus can be like Jesus. And he wants me to trust him to be who he is in and through me. "If we live by the Spirit, let us also walk by the Spirit" (Gal. 5:25). We received him by faith for salvation, and now we can walk in him by faith just the same.

Receiving does not happen automatically in the life of a believer. To receive God's truth in a personal way, you have to let go of the false hiding places and let yourself experience the truth of hiding in his presence. Let the peace of Christ rule in your heart. It sounds easy to say, but feels risky to do. Open your hands, let peace do peace-like work, and watch with hopeful expectation.

BEHIND THE MASK

Ephesians 1 describes the many blessings that belong to us in Christ. Which of these blessings have you been striving after? How do you feel knowing they already belong to you?

What has kept you from receiving your blessings and identity in Christ? What keeps you behind your masks?

What is the difference between obedience to the law and obedience to the truth?

Is there a certain truth that is particularly difficult for you to obey, receive, or to let be true in your life?

In what ways does knowing the difference between your soul and your spirit change the way you think?

Read Philippians 4:6–7. "Be anxious for nothing, but in everything by prayer and supplication with thanksgiving let your requests be made known to God. *And the peace of God, which surpasses all comprehension, will guard your hearts and your minds in Christ Jesus"* (emphasis added). Our hearts and minds are encompassed in our souls, not our spirits. As we let peace rule, it guards our souls. Can you think of a time when you experienced God's peace guarding your soul?

12

remain

on quiet and time

Let the word of Christ richly dwell within you.
—Colossians 3:16

I've never liked the phrase *quiet time* all that much, but I was a good girl who went to Bible college, so I've not always been brave enough to admit it. I never knew what I was supposed to do during a quiet time. Read one verse? Is a chapter enough? Maybe I should memorize the whole book. The list seemed both empty and endless.

There was a depth of intimacy and relevancy missing in my quiet times, but I didn't know what it was for a long time. While I never regretted sitting down and reading my Bible or making myself pray through a list of people, I was often left feeling as though I had *accomplished something* rather than *related with someone*. Jesus does not have bullet points. I cannot check him off. But that is what I tried to do.

When I was in hiding, having a quiet time provided a false sense of security for me. To be found, we must move beyond practicing religion into the reality of truly experiencing Jesus. For me, that sweet transition came in the form of two tiny babies, born seven weeks early.

The Deepening

Being a grown-up was nothing like I thought it would be. Sitting amid a sea of graduates wearing black robes, I considered the internship, the apartment, and the electric bill waiting for me on the other side of the ceremony and wondered when the chancellor would realize she had made an embarrassing mistake. I didn't feel like a grown-up. I wasn't confident or sure. I wasn't steady or strong or emotionally stable. I was a girl wearing a ridiculous hat surrounded by people who knew what they were doing. At least that's what it felt like.

As she called my name to receive that degree, the ring of it sounded strange as it echoed in the coliseum. I wondered when they would realize I was really still a girl with pigtails and skinned knees playing Barbies on the front porch, a girl who had an incredible knack for wasting time and a tendency to cry under pressure.

Still, I confidently walked across that stage, looked the chancellor in the eye, and accepted that empty diploma holder as my own. If there was one thing I learned after four years of college, it was to act confident and sure whether you felt it or not.

A wedding, a honeymoon, and a few years later, I continued to wear that mask of strength and responsibility. Then one day the kid-me showed up again, eyes brimming with tears after months of trying. Test after test was negative, but this one was different: two bright pink lines. The kid was gonna have a baby.

It was several weeks of terrible morning, noon, and night sickness before an ultrasound revealed we were having not one, but two babies. Upon hearing the unexpected, thrilling news, that mask of strength drooped slightly down and to the left. *I'm not sure I can do this.*

Five months later, I caught a glimpse of myself in the reflective metal on the lamp above the operating table—a blurry reflection, but an image nonetheless. The doctors were ready, my man held tightly to my hand, and the babies pushed and waited to burst forth to life. The surgery went well, and out they came—two slippery, whimpering girls bearing the likeness of God and each other. Their mess of a mother was a girl of twenty-seven years who couldn't believe the doctors let her take them home. *Shouldn't a grown-up be in charge of these little lives?*

The transition from normal person to crazy mom was anything but smooth. Their first year was a blurry, watercolor mess of emotion. I was both depressed and elated, an inadequate hero, a shadow disguised as a woman.

That year I learned what it meant to depend on Jesus as my source of life more than I ever had before. It didn't happen at 6:00 a.m. with my coffee and my pen and my cozy blanket by the fire. It happened at 3:00 a.m. with two screaming babies and spit-up running down my leg. Gone were the days of quiet times I had known. I hardly had any time of quiet, much less a quiet time.

Did I read my Bible that year? Sure. Did I pray that year? You'd better believe it. But it began to look different than it had before. My expectations of what it meant to be a grown-up shifted and flipped during that sleepless year. The confident, strong, independent woman I thought I would one day become had disappeared like a vapor, and in her place stood my relevant Jesus, waiting with a smile to be the strength I didn't have on my own.

Being mom to those babies taught me to stop trying to be like Jesus and simply trust Jesus to be himself in and through me. Because the truth was, I couldn't do it.

There is a time for cozy blankets and journals. There is also a time for gut-wrenching, on-your-knees soul searching; for joy unspeakable and peace unwavering and mourning with the ugly cry. Life is fluid, it ebbs and flows in cycles of busy and rest, crisis and joy.

The truth is, I struggled through this shift. I fought it and cried about it and wondered if I could really call myself a Christian since it was so hard to spend any time with God. What I didn't realize until later was just how vital this shift would be in order for me to understand God as he is and not as I think he should be.

We have a Creator who knows about the swing. He set it into motion. He is not afraid of our life stages. They don't hinder him. He is gracious and compassionate, slow to anger and abounding in love. He offers us a new place to hide.

To Be a Woman

We all have an idea of what it means to be a woman. Young good girls have visions of growing up to be a "strong woman of God." We know what she will look like and how she will act in crisis. We know what she will say to those who are hurting and what kind of cookies she will make for her kids. And we know what kind of quiet times she has.

There is a woman in our church who faced unspeakable grief. Her husband died only a few years into their marriage, and she was left with a child to bring up and a heart to mend back together. People referred to this woman from a distance as an amazing example of faith and strength. She was called a strong woman of God. And when I heard that sentence, I wanted to say, "Not anymore."

In the midst of grief, there is no such thing as strong women of God. There is only brokenness, desperate need, and little girls in Daddy's lap. We are not called to be strong women. Oh, how that sentence makes me bristle. I want to be strong, independent, and capable. This broken, desperate need for Christ offends my mask.

He does not think as we do. He does not see our relationship measured by ticking clocks, marked with a time to start and stop. I long to have morning times of uninterrupted quiet. From alarm clock chime to the bottom of my first hot cup, I want quiet and stillness and Jesus. But when I don't get that, I am amazed at how quickly I shift from a woman of good and holy intentions to crazy monster mommy who just wants a few minutes alone to pray. Is that too much to ask? *Is it?*

And then I cuss on the inside.

And stomp off to make their lunches.

And miss the point entirely.

Who Is?

Moses missed the point too. In Exodus 3, we find Moses pasturing his father-in-law's flock when the Lord shows up in a bush on fire. And God calls his name, "Moses, Moses!"

"Here I am." Moses speaks to the bush, perhaps out of reflex from hearing his name. There was no time to consider how or why this impossible thing was happening.

That is when the Lord reveals his holy identity: the God of Abraham, the God of Isaac, and the God of Jacob. He tells Moses that he has not forgotten his people and will deliver them from the hand of the Egyptians. Then, he tells Moses how he plans to do it: "Therefore, come now, and I will send you to Pharaoh, so that you may bring My people, the sons of Israel, out of Egypt" (3:10).

Therefore, come now. The dreaded words of sacrifice. The bridge between how things were and how they will be. The call to move beyond perceived control into a cautious, holy trust.

This is not good news to Moses. He does not hesitate to tell God exactly what he fears as that bush burns hot and loud in front of him.

"Who am I, that I should go to Pharaoh, and that I should bring the sons of Israel out of Egypt?" (3:11).

145

I ask that question a lot. *Who am I?* Who am I that I should parent these little ones? Who am I with no dramatic story of life change? Who am I to think God accepts me just as I am and not as I should be? Who am I?

God answers from that blazing bush. "Certainly I will be with you" (3:12).

But it isn't enough.

Moses moves on to the next question, one that is much more relevant than the first. He admits that he will go to the Israelites and tell them God has sent him, but he wants to know what to tell them when they ask who has sent him. "They may say to me, 'What is His name?' What shall I say to them?" (3:13).

Oh God, who should I tell them you are?

Now this is a relevant question. The question is no longer about Moses. It is no longer *Who am I?* Now he wants to know, *Who is God?*

"God said to Moses, 'I AM WHO I AM' . . . Thus you shall say to the sons of Israel, 'I AM has sent me to you'" (3:14).

What an infuriating answer. Is this a joke? It doesn't even make sense. It isn't even grammatically correct.

And that is precisely the point.

I AM is.

Not just when I have time to sit and soak in the quiet. Not just when I wake up with the dawn and revel in the truth. I AM is my present reality and my only hope of freedom. Certainly, he will be with me.

To Remain

I like to think I have grown past trying to earn my way into God's acceptance. Because of my good girl tendency to perform, I have had a lot of relearning to do when it comes to understanding how to remain in Christ.

In the midst of an active, blurry week, John came home from a walk with a friend who asked him this question: *Are you willing to be more and do less?* The words stopped me in my dinner-making, clothes-washing, nose-wiping tracks. On the scale of life, these days my doing far outweighs my being.

Be more. Do less. It sounds as blissful as it does unrealistic. I hear the mocking voice of reason, the one telling me how the sentiment is nice, but the reality is that things just have to get done. There is no room for rest, for still, for quiet. The words repeat like a drumbeat in the background.

Do. Act. Work. Produce.

The lie creeps back in and I forget to receive the big and the little as from the hand of God. Instead, I try to earn it. I put the demands of life on one side and the time I spend with God on the other and worry and fret when life falls down heavy with a bang. I measure my time spent with God against everything else and let it define me, for better or worse.

And then Jesus enters in and changes everything. In the place of my balance scale, he puts a cross and willingly places his hands on either side. They weigh equal amounts, both hands scarred heavy with the weight of the world. He fulfilled the requirements of the measuring because I couldn't keep the law and was never meant to. All he asks is that I receive his sacrifice for my inadequacy and then stay in that place of truth.

To remain in him means to refuse to get up from his lap. When it seems like the situation calls for me to stand up and take charge, Jesus gives me permission to remain still, if only on the inside, to trust deeply and fully that he will be strong on my behalf. Even when it seems impossible. Even when it's counterintuitive. Even if it means I will look weak. To remain in him means to *let the Great I Am be*. And there is that word again: let. The letting power is still up to you.

> I am the true vine, and my Father is the gardener . . . Remain in me, and I will remain in you. No branch can bear fruit by itself; it must remain in the vine. Neither can you bear fruit unless you remain in me. I am the vine; you are the branches.

If a man remains in me and I in him, he will bear much fruit;
apart from me you can do nothing. (John 15:1–5 NIV)

He is the true vine, the source of nourishment and life to the
branches. The job of the branch is not to make life happen,
but to remain in the vine. To remain in Christ is to stay where
you already are. No need to get up and try to find that which
you already have. Stay. Abide. Remain. Believe.

This is where another voice speaks, the voice of One who
invites you to abide in him and rest. He renews, restores, and
redeems. In the inspired words of Sarah Young, "He bends
time in your favor."[1] In a day that seems impossibly packed
to overflowing with the list, he can multiply time and space
like loaves and fishes beside the sea. And the gentle rhythm
of truth rises from within.

Be. Trust. Receive. Respond.

When I live as though I believe that's true, activity doesn't
stop. Rather, it takes on new life. It doesn't require an entire
day of quiet reflection, although I wouldn't turn it down. It
is purposing in my heart not to fret. It is allowing the day
to go as it will. It is holding my plans with an open hand
and a willing heart. When I have a chance to either be still
or check my email, I can choose to be still. Not every time.
Just this time.

Even in the midst of lots of activity, our souls have permission to rest. I don't always choose rest, but this is a sweet
reminder to me that I have that option.

Stoking the Fire

Earlier I talked about Fil Anderson's book, *Breaking the
Rules*. Fil also happens to be a family friend. We invited
him to share his thoughts on spending time with God with
our students in the youth group. He shared a story of sitting
with his wife on the couch one evening, enjoying their newly
emptied nest. When the movie was over, he suggested they

sleep on the floor in front of the fire rather than heading off to bed. His wife Lucie's only hesitancy was that she didn't want to wake up in the morning to a cold room and a fire that had long since gone out. Fil convinced her to do it only after he promised to wake up periodically and stoke the fire to keep it going.

He likened this fire stoking to time spent with God. He didn't put the fire out and make a brand-new one every hour. He merely kept the same one going, moving embers and logs around to catch the flame in new ways so the warm kept on warming.

Quiet time is no longer something I do. Rather, it is a description of what happens when I am with God. Time can be a loud, chaotic, rushing-around companion. But as I sit in the presence of God, he quiets my time. Now that I know what the truth is, I long to allow space for my soul and spirit to begin to believe it.

There is great value, beauty, and rest to be found in spending time and being quiet with the Lord of the Universe. It is vital to see it for what it is: the continuation of connection, a deepening of relationship, and permission to rest, like keeping an already hot fire hot.

To Dwell

To remain in him means both to sit with him and to walk with him, to literally let the peace of Christ reduce the noise of worry and the clatter of chaos so that we can receive truth. In the same way we receive the peace of Christ and let it rule in our hearts, we are to let the Word of God dwell richly within us. When I hear that, I picture reading the Bible and putting it to memory. A quiet time. A study. An external catalyst. This is how it starts out. But we can't stop there, because it is so much more than that.

In Colossians 3:16, the Greek word for dwell is *enoikeō*, which literally means "to dwell in" or "to live in."[2] Kenneth S.

Wuest wrote a commentary on the book of Colossians and in reference to this verse he says this: "[The believer] is to so yield himself to the Word that there is a certain at-homeness of the Word in his being. The Word should be able to feel at home in his heart . . . The Holy Spirit uses the Word of God that we know as He talks to us and guides our lives. He can efficiently talk to us to the extent to which we know the Word. That is the language He uses."[3]

I love seeing the Word capitalized here because it reminds me of John 1, where the disciple whom Jesus loved speaks of his Lord as the Word: "In the beginning was the Word, and the Word was with God, and the Word was God. He was in the beginning with God" (vv. 1–2).

We cannot separate the written Word of God from the person of Jesus Christ. God's Spirit indwells us in the same way we are to let his Word dwell richly within us. It is not only remaining in Christ; it is letting Christ remain in you. It is not only memorizing Scripture and having a Bible study; it is letting the person of Jesus Christ take up residence within you, not as a timid houseguest, but as the abundant provider, the bread-winner, the respected head of the household, the host. He doesn't sit at your table, feeble and frail, waiting for you to feed him by reading your Bible and praying. He stands strong at the head, graciously filling your plate with all that he is. He lavishes us with a godly inheritance. The riches of the fruit of his Spirit are made available to us in abundant supply.

It brings new meaning to John 15:5, which we read earlier but I will say again: "If you remain in me and I in you, you will bear much fruit; apart from me you can do nothing." Perhaps the opposite of this is also true: *with me, you can do anything*. "I can do all things through Him who strengthens me" (Phil. 4:13).

We have spent a lot of time talking about what it means to receive truth from Christ and to remain in him, letting his peace rule and his Word dwell richly. So what is to be the result? This is where it gets exciting. This is where the world gets to see God through the hands and feet and hearts of true believers. This is where the masks become a blurry memory and Jesus shows up in mighty, God-sized ways: in true worship and authentic service.

⟨◦⟩ BEHIND THE MASK ⟨◦⟩

When I was in high school and college, having a quiet time sometimes left me feeling as if I had accomplished something rather than related with a person. I equate it to working out: I don't do it very often, but when I do I feel better about myself and slightly superior to those who may not have done the same that day. Have you ever been able to relate to this perspective of a quiet time?

Do you feel like a grown-up yet? In what ways has your perspective of time with the Lord changed as you have grown up?

God told Moses to tell the Israelites that I AM sent him. Read these synonyms for the word *remain*: stay put, stay behind, linger, wait, hang about, continue, endure, and hang on. These are all present, right-now words, much like the way God referred to himself with Moses. Does knowing that I AM *is right now* make any difference in the way you think about the course of your day?

13

* * * * * * * * * * * * *

respond

on worship and service

Whatever you do in word or deed, do all in the name of the
Lord Jesus, giving thanks through Him to God the Father.

—Colossians 3:17

*A*s a good girl, my worship was small and my service
was toxic because I didn't understand the completeness of my rescue. I knew I was going to heaven when I died,
but I thought my life on earth was all up to me. Jesus saved me,
and now he was standing back with his arms crossed, waiting to see how I would live my life. Service seemed a burden.
Worship felt contrived. I had received Christ by faith for my
salvation, but I was working hard for the rest. Until he said
enough. When I began to understand that my true identity
was not in how I looked, how I felt, or the lies I believed, my
masks began to lose their staying power. It wasn't because I

was trying hard to remove them. It was because I was seeing Jesus for who he really is, and in turn I was letting him see me.

And so what happens in the life of a believer who has received both the gift of salvation *and* the knowledge of Christ's everyday presence and empowering? What is the result of sticking to his side like a girl peering out from the folds of her mama's dress? What happens when a mask-wearing good girl comes out of hiding and dares to trust love rather than be pushed around by fear? I love the way Paul describes it in Colossians 2:6–7:

> And now, just as you accepted Christ Jesus as your Lord [receive for salvation], you must continue to follow him [receive for the daily bread]. Let your roots grow down into him, and let your lives be built on him [remain]. Then your faith will grow strong in the truth you were taught, and you will overflow with thankfulness [respond]. (NLT)

To receive is to let. To remain is to let. But after that, the verse simply describes what will be if we *let* the first two things. Our faith *will grow strong* and we *will overflow with thankfulness* as we receive from and remain in him. The action and the struggle are in the receiving and remaining. As we dare to believe what is true and decide to remain in that truth, faith and thankfulness will be the natural response. And like the Virgin Mary, who chose to believe the angel and remain in that truth, worship flows naturally out.

Mary did not have to work hard to muster up an appropriate response to the gift she was given. She did not wring her hands with furrowed brow, wondering if she was doing enough to earn the right to be the mother of the Lord. She did not look over her shoulder to see what the neighbors would think of her. She did not fake happy and joy while trembling with fear on the inside.

Instead, Mary rose up and hurried to the hill country to visit her cousin Elizabeth. Action springs forth from the heart of a woman who has encountered God. At the sight of her, the unborn baby inside Elizabeth leaped with joy. Elizabeth herself was filled up with the Holy Spirit and cried out blessings on Mary, the appropriate response upon seeing one who has been with the Lord. And worship and joy burst forth from Mary, a young woman who literally received Jesus into her body and remained, unwavering, in the truth.

> My soul exalts the Lord,
> And my spirit has rejoiced in God my Savior.
> For He has had regard for the humble state of His bondslave;
> For behold, from this time on all generations will count me blessed.
> For the Mighty One has done great things for me;
> And holy is His name. (Luke 1:46–49)

Living Worship

We toss the word *worship* around in our churched-people groups, in hand-folding fellowship, in reference to the building where church happens. We have worship teams, worship songs, worship bands, and even special worship services.

It's kind of weird when you think about it. Maybe you stand side-by-side with closed-eyed strangers in too-high heels with hymnals or screens or drums. Perhaps you sing with a guitar in a house, sitting small and comfy on the very couch where you watched *Survivor* last Thursday. Either way, singing songs about sin and blood and Jesus and the cross is strange. If I try to see it all from the perspective of someone who doesn't believe in God, it gets me all messed up. Because it's weird is what it is.

We refer to church as a building, and we use worship as a noun: "Did you go to worship this morning?" Or, if we use it as a verb, we refer to the kind of worship that comes in the form of melodies and rhythms, with voices and strumming and notes. God never intended for us to refer to church as a building. And he never intended worship to be reduced to a church service. His church is his people, and worship is what they do.

When you're used to wearing a mask, you are comfortable with compartmentalizing life. Mask-wearing good girls put worship in a slivered-up pie chart, dividing our lives into segments of importance. We assign percentages for work, service, prayer, school, exercise, PTA, meal planning, bill paying, dog walking, toilet cleaning, church, and rest (if we're lucky). But the woman who has freely received the abundance of truth from Jesus abides in that truth as her very life. In other words, the lines of the pie chart disappear, and worship covers the full circle. Free women respond with worship in everything. It is a natural outpouring of thankfulness and awareness of love and grace and truth. It isn't mustered up; it flows out.

We breathe in air and breathe out worship. We receive love and extend worship. We embrace children, offering worship. We comfort, we laugh, we mourn, we dance, we read, we dream, we exist—all worship. We pay the bills, we run on the treadmill, we enjoy a good movie, we make dinner, we welcome friends with open arms—worship, all worship. We send money and offer prayer and sit with a lonely neighbor, in Jesus' name. We wait for love, we long for home, we pour out our hearts and hopes and fears and longing; we create with words and photos and colors and food, all beautiful acts of worship.

But we don't call it that.

We call those things *living*. But when the Spirit of the living God lives inside of you, then your living is also your worship. What else would it be? "Therefore I urge you, brethren, by the mercies of God, to present your bodies a living and holy sacrifice, acceptable to God, which is your spiritual service of worship" (Rom. 12:1). "And whatever you do [no matter what it is] in word or deed, do everything in the name of the Lord Jesus and in [dependence upon] His Person, giving praise to God the Father through Him" (Col. 3:17 AMP). When we depend on Jesus, when we know we can't but he can, we worship. It is so much bigger than we let it be. When we let peace rule, we worship. When we let his Word dwell richly within us, we worship. When we receive the gifts in life, both small and big, as from his hand, we offer worship.

The Glory

I attended two different colleges after high school. I've mentioned the first, Columbia Bible College in South Carolina. The second was the University of North Carolina at Greensboro. While at Bible college, I majored in music and studied the Bible. A lot. The work was hard, much harder than you might imagine. My grades were fair, but they were not as good as they had been in high school.

My sophomore year, I discovered that piano had a lot to do with math. And math is the bane of my existence. I have nightmares about math, ones where I can't get my locker open, I've lost my math textbook, and I run through the empty halls of my high school looking for my math class. I didn't love piano or the theory of piano enough to make a life of it, so I transferred to UNCG to study educational interpreting for the Deaf. I loved every minute of it. In fact, except for one class, I made straight A's my entire time there. That one exception was biology.

Biology was difficult for me. I am more of an English and history girl. I took the most basic math class required by my major, which is the only reason I was able to squeeze an A out of it. But biology was a different entity. While people are endlessly fascinating to me, organisms leave me stumped.

But it was in biology where I learned about the ways our human body works. It was there where I learned how my blood circulates through my body a thousand times every day, and it made me think about how I can't will it to happen. This heart of mine keeps pumping on, and it isn't because I wrote it in my planner. My body worships without my permission. I was created to glorify God. And so his creation displays his glory, even in the ones who don't give him the credit. Their very existence breathes the breath of their Creator, and they walk around smart-like and arrogant, like little emperors without their clothes.

Isaiah 42:8 says this: "I am the LORD; that is My name; I will not give My glory to another, nor My praise to graven images." The God who sees us, the God who rescues us, and the God who knows us better than we know ourselves will not share the glory with any man. This new kind of hiding means that it isn't all about my dysfunction anymore. Because the truth is, the mask-wearing good girl is all about herself. In her most secret place, she wants the glory. But it is only in him that we have been made complete.

Now, I am hidden with Christ in God. It is my good-looking, hard-working, boot-strap-pulling, religious self that strives for glory and credit. Now, as I receive Jesus as my very life and remain in him, I can step off that performance treadmill and ascribe worth to the Creator and Sustainer of the world and everything in it. Now, I hide in the completeness of Christ. I rest in his shadow. I am hidden, but not behind a paper mask of false identities and try-hard religion. Now, I am hidden in Christ: safe, secure, and complete. And when I hide in him, it is no longer I but Christ who is seen.

Remember, I have died. The old me with her old ways who wants glory and credit. The mask is still there, but that is my flesh. My identity, or my spirit, has been made new in Christ. "I have been crucified with Christ; and it is no longer I who live, but Christ lives in me" (Gal. 2:20).

Hearing the Music

After I graduated, I worked for several years as a sign language interpreter in the public school system. The student I interpreted for was an attractive, well-liked athlete. Though she had a few friends who used sign language with her, I interpreted most every interaction she had with teachers and classmates, as she never used her own voice.

For the most part, I enjoyed my role as the sign language interpreter. It allowed me to have an eye and ear into situations I would never have otherwise been invited to: private counseling sessions, high school girlfriend talk, basketball team huddles, and lots of others. But there were some things for which interpreting was nearly impossible. Rap music at a pep-rally, for example. Even if I could have understood the words, it went way too fast. But the words mattered little. It was the music that moved people. I could have told her music was playing, but she didn't need me to. She could see evidence of that fact in each one of her peers. Every person with working ears couldn't help but respond to the music.

Hearing people assume details about people who are Deaf, like they can all read lips or they can interpret details of the music as it vibrates in their seat. The truth is, though she could feel the fact that music was playing, she didn't need to try to decipher the beat. All she had to do was watch her classmates move around her and follow their lead. If I hadn't known she was Deaf, I would have assumed she was responding to the music just like everyone around her. But the truth was, she couldn't hear anything. She was watching and imitating, responding to her environment.

Good girls are like Deaf girls dancing. We know what to say, how to say it, and what to do to convince people we are doing this Christian thing right. From the outside, you may not be able to tell the difference between a girl ridden with guilt and a girl freed by grace. But there is an overwhelming difference between the two. Good girls see Jesus as someone to copy. Free women listen to the voice of his Spirit who dwells inside us.

When you think of responding to Jesus this way, it is hard to tell the difference between worship and service. They are both a natural response to the love of God; they are both a direct result of listening to his voice.

When Jesus Wears Nikes

Worship and service are the result of knowing the truth about our new identity in Christ. Contrary to what the critics might say, understanding our new identity as believers is not a passive teaching focused on self. It is the very path by which Jesus is able to show up in our lives.

But trusting Jesus in this way can't simply be a declaration of what I believe to be true. It has to have hands and feet. Sometimes my faith has to risk getting dirty and being ordinary. That simply happens in the everyday, living-life things. The mystery of Christ in you can be so easily overlooked because at first, it doesn't look mysterious.

I mentioned before how our youth group does a service project every summer to walk alongside local churches in different cities and serve where there is a need. They spent several summers in Gulfport, Mississippi, after Hurricane Katrina devastated the Gulf Coast in the summer of 2005. After he had been gone several days on this particular trip, John called me on the phone after a long day of service work.

The trip was a hard one for him, and not just because the town was so devastated by the storm. He had been hired as the youth pastor only weeks before he left. It was his first summer with this group of students and volunteer leaders. All two hundred faces were new to him. As we spoke that night, he shared with me the worn-down, insecure place where he was. The weather was sweltering. He felt lonely. He had not yet learned many names. But in that place of desperation, he discovered a sweet invitation to trust Jesus to work in and through him in that place. Even though I couldn't see his face, I could tell he was smiling when he said, "Today, Jesus wears Nikes and a Callaway golf hat."

Today, Jesus wears a ponytail and washes the dirty dishes.
Today, Jesus wears scrubs and comforts the family.
Today, Jesus wears a suit and balances the budget.
Today, Jesus wears a smile as he makes the bed.

Today, Jesus.

That is when "Christ in you, the hope of glory" becomes a reality and not just a verse. Because where is Jesus' influence on earth if not through us? How else do we live out the life of Christ if not through our everyday, mundane tasks? "Whatever you do in word or deed, do all in the name of the Lord Jesus, giving thanks through Him to God the Father" (Col. 3:17).

From this perspective, worship and service are not disciplines we practice in order to earn something or to pay him back out of obligation. Rather, worship and service are the natural responses of a girl fulfilled by love, compelled to look beyond herself.

Behind the Mask

Is it difficult for you to imagine your living as worship? Why or why not?

Have you ever felt like a Deaf girl dancing when it comes to worship and service?

Read Mary's Magnificat in Luke 1:46–55. How would you describe her posture, her feelings, and her countenance? What types of things was she *not* thinking about during this outpouring of worship?

14

remember

on setting your mind

Set your mind on the things above, not on the things that are on earth.

—Colossians 3:2

When I was younger, I wrote in my Bible a lot. I liked to use different colors and write notes along the side. I grew up watching my mom write in her Bible and kind of thought that's what you were supposed to do. Sometime in college, I stopped. I can't say for sure why, but I think the underlined verses became somewhat of a distraction for me.

A few days ago, I watched as John underlined something in his Bible and then wrote a note in the margins about it. I couldn't stop myself from asking him why. "What if the Lord wants to reveal something new and different to you but you can't hear it because you've written in the margin your note about what you heard today?"

He looked at me without a hint of defense. "Or what if he wants to remind me of something I already know?"

I couldn't argue with that. So much of walking with Jesus is about remembering that which has already been revealed. Jesus loves me, this I know. But oh, how often I forget.

Rewired to Be Reminded

Aside from *Extreme Makeover: Home Edition*, I also really like to watch TLC's *What Not to Wear*. The hosts, Stacy London and Clinton Kelly, take ordinary people who don't know how to dress for their body type. Then, they teach them. They get new clothes and new hairdos, basically a whole new look. (Raise your hand if you see a makeover-show-watching pattern here).

There was one episode in particular that featured a woman named Sarah. Sarah was a cancer survivor who, during the year the show was taped, also lost ninety pounds. She had a double mastectomy and was forced to learn how to live in a body very different from the one she was accustomed to. While the hosts originally thought her body image struggle was because of the double mastectomy, they quickly realized that was only part of the issue. Even though Sarah had lost ninety pounds, when she looked in the mirror she still saw herself as overweight. Her mind had not yet caught up with her reality.

And then she said this: "I wish I could open my brain, rewire myself, close it back up, and I'd be good." I thought about that for a long time after she said it, because I need rewiring too. My mind has not yet caught up with my reality.

The reality is I am safe.

My mind still lives in fear.

The reality is I am loved.

My mind still races to find ways to ensure my acceptance.

The reality is I have worth.

My mind dwells on thoughts of self-hatred.

So how can I get my mind to line up with my reality? To act differently I must think differently. Until my beliefs change, my mask will stay on tight. My mind needs to be rewired.

We may have learned to hold our tongue, to raise our hands in worship, to be kind when we feel unkind. We may have learned to act right. But the unseen mind is an unruly battlefield. Even though I know that my spirit has now been united with God's Spirit and my true identity is found there, my soul still has muscle memory. I am a believer, but I am still aware of the flesh within me, that part of me that tries to get my own needs met. For the good girl, the process of me getting my own needs met tends to look pretty good from the outside, as the previous chapters can attest. In fact, it seems as though the tendency in our culture is to move people from doing the bad things to doing the good things, or from having a negative self-image to a positive self-image. But God doesn't support either of those systems. He wants us to have a biblical self-image. And the only way to do that is to shift our dependence from self onto God. The key to that transition is found in setting our minds.

Setting Our Minds

My sister-in-law is one of the most joy-filled people I have ever known. Her smile exudes life. Her laugh is infectious. Her excitement over small gifts is one of the things I most love about her. Susan loves the ocean. She loves to bike and walk and soak it all in. One of her favorite things to do there is to look for sand dollars. As she is walking, it's not uncommon for her to actually pray for the Lord to show her just one. And when she finds that one, she is thrilled and thankful.

A few weeks ago, I sat with Susan on the beach as we watched my kids play in the water. One of them found a sand dollar, and she jumped up in excitement with them. A treasure! Found! They were so excited. A young girl was watching from a distance, bucket in hand, suit sagging in back. She walked over to us, smiled, and said, "Do you wanna know a secret?" She continued to explain that the sand dollars were everywhere; you just have to know where to look. I glanced up and down the beach as she talked, the smooth sand wet and reflective during low tide. I was skeptical of her secret, as I didn't see even one sand dollar. But she continued to explain if you look for five little holes in the sand and dig just a little, that is where they will be.

My kids quickly got to work, walking and searching. It didn't take long. Suddenly, that five-hole pattern appeared everywhere. They would find it, dig a little, and pull out their treasure. A sand dollar! They were indeed everywhere, literally covering the beach. You just had to know where to look.

It took a little bit of work, the digging. But the digging did not make the sand dollars exist. The sand dollars were already there. They were hiding just under the surface. As a good girl, I often find myself trying to work to earn acceptance from God, as if it isn't there already and my work will somehow produce it.

I think of all the gifts we have been given in Christ. Our fruitless, worn-out efforts to follow him often look like our running around on an empty beach, looking for the gift on the surface of the sand and becoming discouraged when we discover there is nothing there. But the truth is, we need not run around so much. We simply need to stop, dig a little, and there it is. That digging effort is what it means to set our minds. "And do not be conformed to this world, but be transformed by the renewing of your mind, so that you may prove what the will of God is, that which is good and acceptable and perfect" (Rom. 12:2).

Setting, or renewing, our minds is where transformation happens. Our spirits have already been made alive, but our minds have not yet caught up. We have to decide with our wills to teach our minds about *what is already true in Christ*. We cannot simply recycle old patterns of belief. We must find new ones.

New Patterns

When I don't set my mind, my mind sets itself. It's like when I'm working and actively engaged on my laptop, the screen does what I tell it to do. But if I walk away and leave it to its own devices, the screen saver will eventually begin to run. The same thing happens in my mind. If I don't actively set it, it will inactively switch into default mode. And my default setting is shame.

Shame says I should be doing whatever it is I'm not doing, or I should be whatever it is I'm not. So if I'm doing the laundry, I worry I should have already done the dishes, and then I feel shame for not being a better multitasker. If I'm cleaning the kids' rooms, I feel guilty for not teaching them how to do it themselves and then shame sets in for being a bad mother. Sometimes I can't even put my finger on what it is that caused the shame in the first place. I simply realize after a few days that I have been walking around under a cloud of discouragement and I can't seem to shake it away. Those clouds of discouragement show up when we forget to remember to set our minds.

Your default setting may not be shame. Yours may be anger, fear, worry, resentment, anxiety, or indifference. And when our default setting is activated, we reach for those masks to cover them up. I feel shame, so I grab a mask of productivity or strength and get to work. I completely bypass the Spirit within me. I live life on a soul and body level, basing everything I believe on what I can see, touch, taste, smell, and feel.

When I don't set my mind on truth, my mind automatically sinks into shame. And shame opens wide the door to fear. It is so crafty, this fear, that I take it on as my very identity: *I am afraid*, I hear myself say. And in the saying, I practice the presence of fear, rather than rest in the safety of God. I practice my identity as *one who is afraid*, rather than set my mind on the truth of my salvation, as *one who has been given a spirit of power, love, and a sound mind.*

The soul screams, but the Spirit whispers.
Fear shouts for me to run.
The Spirit beckons me, *Come.*
Fear pushes me to hide, take cover, and protect myself.
The Spirit whispers, *I have already overcome.*
Fear hurls insults, chaos, and anxiety.
The Spirit lavishes love, steadfastness, and peace.

It takes work to set our minds on truth. It does not come naturally; it comes supernaturally as we depend on Christ to remind us of truth that is already true, to call to our minds the reality of the victory he has won. I think here of the word *recollect*. Picture a girl with her arms full of small packages, too many to hold all at once. When they topple and fall all around her, she stoops down and scoops them all back up, literally re-collecting all the gifts that are already hers. To set your mind is to recollect truth that already belongs to you. "For the mind set on the flesh is death, but the mind set on the Spirit is life and peace" (Rom. 8:6). The mind set on fear, worry, anger, hurt, revenge, lust, jealousy, and shame is death, but the mind set on the Spirit is life and peace.

Haven or Prison?

What you believe about God and yourself and the world becomes your hiding place. If what you believe is true, then where you live and breathe is a safe place. But what if the things you believe about God and yourself and the world are untrue? Then the place where you hide is decidedly unsafe.

Just because we feel safe where we hide does not mean we are safe. I feel safe behind my mask, not because it's always comfortable, but more because the alternative is unknown. To step out from behind that mask is to risk exposure and rejection. That is why I stay there.

It is only when the haven I thought my mask provided begins to crumble that I will be willing to consider the possibility that perhaps it isn't as safe as I once believed. Our hiding places can be either our havens or our prisons. Setting our minds on the truth of God's Word will ensure that we don't stay captive behind those tattered, tired-out masks. And we will then say with confidence, "You are my hiding place; You preserve me from trouble; You surround me with songs of deliverance" (Ps. 32:7).

Behind the Mask

What is the difference between a positive self-image, a negative self-image, and a biblical self-image?

If we don't set our minds on truth, they will automatically be set on untruth. What is your mind's default screen saver? Fear? Worry? Self-importance? Shame?

Are you willing to receive your abilities from him and release your inabilities to him? How can setting your mind encourage you in doing this?

Do you ever get the sense that the place where you are hiding is unsafe? What keeps you from coming out? Consider the words of the psalmist: "He who dwells in the shelter of the Most High will rest in the shadow of the Almighty" (Ps. 91:1 NIV). In your daily life, are you experiencing rest as you walk with Jesus, or do you feel like you are stumbling behind just trying to keep up?

PART 3

the freedom of being found

For you died, and your life is now hidden with Christ in God.

—Colossians 3:3 NIV

One Fourth of July when my kids were very small, we decided not to go downtown to watch the big fireworks. Instead, we had some fun in the backyard with smoke bombs. They are small, cheap, and unassuming. If you're looking for a pop or a bang, they are pretty useless. But for my preschoolers, they were certainly entertaining. All they do is make lots and lots of smoke. Watching those smoke bombs light from a spark and then fog up the yard in a matter of seconds, I thought about the crazy way our minds work sometimes.

I thought of how one of my girls recently came to me in a moment of four-year-old panic and blurted out, "I don't like these clothes, my face is wrong, and I don't want to have that smile." Well, then.

My face is wrong? Are you kidding me? She's four. How can her face be wrong? Her face couldn't be more right. I

169

thought of how dramatic she was being. How irrational. How ridiculous.

And how painfully familiar.

She sounded just like me. She was simply brave enough to say it out loud. I feel bad about myself just like she does. I feel insecure and listen to the voice in my head that says I'm not good enough or don't measure up. It starts like a spark in my mind, quickly ignites, and fogs up the truth. The emotions burst forth from their familiar hiding place and run around aimlessly, untamed and unruly.

The smoke bombs will go off. The sparks will come. The emotions will swing from high to low. That is normal, neutral even. The challenge comes in knowing what to do in the midst of the smoke, in remembering that my identity is secure in Christ even if my emotions imply otherwise, and in setting my mind on truth even when it doesn't seem to make sense.

We saw in chapter 10 how dangerous it is for God's children to forget truth. Eve was made in the image of God, but she didn't remember. When faced with the liar himself, she couldn't recollect what was true about her. And so often, neither can we. As good girls, it is generally easy to resist the big stuff. The challenge comes in the everyday, living-life things. When the truth doesn't *feel* true is when we begin to believe it isn't. Satan's biggest, most effective weapon against good girls may not be lust or slander or adultery or addiction. It is forgetfulness.

In the remaining chapters, we will discuss what it means to have our lives hidden with Christ in God and how to be convinced of safety even when fear, failure, and feelings get in the way. Instead of reaching for those familiar masks to hide behind, what would it look like to release those masks and believe in our safety without them? Remembering may not be easy, but it is most definitely possible.

15

safe, even when it hurts

Anyone who holds on to life just as it is destroys that life. But
if you let it go, reckless in your love, you'll have it forever,
real and eternal.

—John 12:25 Message

*P*olly's head fell off exactly two days after Christmas. Imagine the scene in our house with two four-year-old girls and one headless Polly Pocket. I had no choice but to fire up the hot glue gun and repair her the best I could. In the end, they had to settle for a Polly with a lopsided head and a vicious neck scar.

When things break, something happens inside us. The routine is interrupted by the urgent, and the broken thing becomes top priority. Shake it. Tap it. Turn it upside down. Find the glue. Replace the batteries. Pull out the needle and thread. Return it to the store. Throw it away.

It isn't natural to just let the broken thing be broken. Ultimately, I have three options: repair it, replace it, or ignore it.

171

But what if the broken thing is a sense of not measuring up or a relationship that has run its course or the death of a dear friend? What if it's a body that refuses to get pregnant even with a heart that wants nothing more? Or a dream that was once bright and glittery but now sits gray and dusty at your feet? Those things can't be as easily repaired, replaced, or ignored.

Closure

I am constantly looking for closure. When I make my to-do lists, I precede each item with a little, hollow box. When the task is completed—the letter sent, the laundry folded, the dishes cleaned—I take great delight in filling in the little box with ink.

I bet you have a system too. Maybe you are an old-school check mark person. Or perhaps you are more bold and like to completely cross through your finished tasks. Whatever your system looks like, I would venture to say that it has one goal: *completion*.

I was talking with a friend who mentioned she was glad a certain tumultuous relationship had ended, but now she just wanted some closure. It reminded me of an episode of *Friends* where Rachel had been secretly in love with Ross. On a particularly difficult night of realizing she may never be able to be with him, she called him up and left a message on his answering machine, telling him she was over him and ending with, "And that is what they call *closure.*" It was funny because she was so obviously not over him. But she desperately wanted closure, some way to close the door on her broken heart.

I began to consider the word *closure*, the idea of closing up a relationship, or of ending it in a way that is satisfying and makes sense. I think of tightening the lid on a jar and putting it away, of taping up a box and storing it in the attic, of coloring in a little, hollow box on my to-do list.

Is closure really possible when it comes to relationships? I would prefer that to be true, because closure implies that I will no longer have to deal with the thing I have closed. I'm not saying some aspects of closure aren't needed and even necessary in the ending of relationships. But more often what we really seek is healing.

Healing is messy and fluid and often unpredictable. I can't manufacture my own healing. It usually takes longer than I think, runs deeper than I wished, and involves more areas of my life than I ever imagined. But once I come through it on the other side, healing not only offers the closure I thought I wanted, it comes with a wholeness, wellness, and restoration that closure lacks.

Broken Relationship

We were eighteen and I was going to marry him. We met the first semester of our senior year in high school. It was a small Christian school in a suburb of Detroit. I was the new girl with a southern accent, and he was the poetic musician with the perfect amount of brood.

We were friends first, but as time went on, I began to see him as more than that. I loved him as much as I knew about love. When I compare that to what I know now, it wasn't much. But I loved how I felt when I was with him. Beautiful. Wanted. Worth fighting for.

He was a good guy. We were respectful of one another. We encouraged each other in our faith. We did things right, for the most part. We made plans and had forever dreams and shared fancy words.

Fancy words are intimacy for the good girl, and those beautiful words and someday dreams became a great source of security for me. They also led me to believe that this boy knew me better than he actually did and allowed me to fool myself into thinking I was as good as I looked on paper.

We grew up some and went to different faraway colleges where time and distance had their way with us. When our relationship ended, something broke. I broke. I made vain attempts to manufacture closure by staying strong and putting up a good front. I mentally sifted through my closet of masks and pulled out the ones labeled *strong* and *resilient*.

I didn't cry after our breakup. Not for a long time. I tried my best to repair my heart on my own. When that didn't work, I ignored the pain. When that stopped working, I eased the pain with another boy who liked me. I didn't see any other option.

To enter into brokenness is not natural. To face the broken things and allow them to be broken doesn't even make the list of things I would choose. It didn't feel right to allow myself to grieve the loss of the friendship, the relationship, and mostly, the dream. It felt selfish, indulgent, and wrong. So I avoided the pain and forged on, headfirst into another relationship that was doomed before it even began.

The Haunting

I have tried to think of a more appropriate word to describe what happened in the years after the nonhealing of this high school relationship. The only accurate term is *haunting*.

Several years went by. I dated a boy who was great, but after a year or so, that relationship inevitably ended too. I then had some time with no boys, some time of rediscovery and solitary focus. When I met the man who is now my husband, I knew right away there was something about him. When a friend introduced us, I could hardly look him in the eye, afraid he might notice the attraction I already felt. As the months went by and I got to know him better, he undid me. He was the one I was waiting for. His was the voice I most wanted to hear. It was a dream come true to have this man love me. And marrying him two years later was a joy. We had been married for a only a short time when my past began to show up again.

While sorting through some boxes, I came across an old letter this former boyfriend wrote me during our senior year.

Before long, he was simply there, hovering in the background of my mind. It bothered me that I would think of him. I began to question why. I was married, happy, in love. Why was he showing up in this most random way? And then the lies began to weave their way in . . .

What a horrible wife you are. What a horrible person. If anyone knew, if anyone found out that he is showing up in your thoughts . . . Why are you thinking of him? You had better keep this to yourself. And so I did. For a while.

As embarrassing as it was, I felt compelled to tell John, not because I thought it necessarily meant anything about our marriage, but because I needed a way to talk through what was happening. I finally visited a counselor. When I began to share with him about these thoughts of my former boyfriend, his first question to me was surprising: *How did the relationship end?*

I hadn't considered it. After all this time, the consequences of the mask wearing had finally caught up with me. Because I had never properly grieved the loss of that friendship or acknowledged the pain that it caused, healing had not yet happened. Even after all those years. And my desperate need for it snuck up on me through the back door of my mind.

The fact that I needed healing did not mean I was horrible; it meant I was human. We all share a common frailty, but the good girl won't let me take part. She has both held me back from facing weakness and shoved me forward to fake strong.

Where there is no healing, there is often a haunting. To escape the haunting, we will do one of two things: find a mask or find a healer.

Falling to the Ground

The thing about healing is sometimes it has to get bad before it gets better. It can almost feel like a death, this letting go and sitting in the broken. When I stop to think about it, nearly everything I do is to prevent death in one way or another. I

175

wear my seat belt. I schedule a yearly physical. I look both ways when I cross the street. I eat bananas. I even work out sometimes.

It's not just my body that needs maintenance. Everything needs to be kept up in order to prevent decay: the car, the house, the yard, and the appliances. We hire experts and buy insurance to make sure our belongings are functioning properly. They are no use to us if they break.

I try to prevent other kinds of death, too. The kind not related with the body but connected to the soul. My husband and I schedule date nights to keep our relationship fresh and engaged. I spend time with my kids to maintain a heart connection. I call my mom and my sister almost every day to hear how they are, to laugh at silly things, to keep our relationship moving and living. I cannot think of a situation where I would choose death on purpose.

Perhaps that is why Jesus' words sometimes sound so foreign. I secretly wonder if my Bible has a typo. In John 12:24, Jesus says that a grain of wheat remains alone and useless unless it falls to the ground and dies. Everything in me fights the concept of falling to the ground and dying. It sounds like surrender, like giving up and letting go. It fights against every inclination I've been taught to value. To fall to the ground and die means I'm done and it's over and there's nothing else I can do.

Falling to the ground is for the weak. Falling to the ground is for those who can't handle things. Falling to the ground is not an option. It is the good girl's ultimate fear, and I avoid it at all costs.

That is, until I have no other choice.

And so, that is what taking off our masks often looks like: Jesus bringing us to the place where we have to choose what we will believe.

Before he talked about wheat in John 12, Jesus talked about bread in John 6. "I am the living bread that came down from heaven. If anyone eats of this bread, he will live forever. This bread is my flesh, which I will give for the life of the world" (John 6:51 NIV).

This statement caused many of Jesus' followers to turn away. When faced with the choice to believe that he was the source of eternal life or to depend on what they knew, they chose to walk away. So Jesus turned to his disciples and asked them if they wanted to leave, too. Simon Peter's response brings me to tears every time I read it: "Lord, to whom shall we go? You have the words of eternal life. We believe and know that you are the Holy One of God" (John 6:68–69 NIV).

I cry for two reasons. First, because I wonder myself where else I would go if it weren't for these words of eternal life, if it weren't for this God-Man who came to walk on earth for me and who died and rose again, all for me. The second reason I tear up is because I know Simon Peter's story. I know what is coming after he says these words. I know he *will* go somewhere else, he *will* revert back to fear, he *will* deny the Holy One of God. But I also know his story doesn't end there. We'll talk more about Peter in the next chapter.

Jesus brings his people to the edge of self-sufficiency and urges us to fall to the ground in surrender. I hold on to my kernel of wheat because with it I believe I have life. And that hard, outer shell is like the mask I wear to make life work. What I don't know is that when that kernel falls to the ground and is subjected to the elements of rain and soil and heat and light, that shell will break and burst forth with life. The life is inside but the shell keeps it hidden.

To avoid the fall often means living a less-than life. To hold on to upright might mean I keep my carefully crafted reputation, but it also means living in fear of being found out. We have a God who stands on his head, who does things backwards from the natural way of things. "Blessed are the poor in spirit, for theirs is the kingdom of heaven. Blessed are those who mourn, for they shall be comforted. Blessed are the gentle, for they will inherit the earth" (Matt. 5:3–5).

Broken in Death

Brandy was one of those girlfriends who never seemed to change. Even when we liked the same boy in the tenth grade, we didn't fight or hate each other. Instead we laughed and cried about it in the school bathroom during lunch. We both made the JV cheerleading squad that same year, and our friendship grew. Her dad had a pool where we hung out a lot. She liked to make mixtapes.

There were six other girls we were close with as well, and we did silly things together like getting professional photos done as a group and calling ourselves the Great Eight. Brandy was always supportive, kind, and upbeat. She was a good friend.

As often happens with good high school friends, we didn't keep in touch very well after graduation. So when I received the news of her engagement, I was excited to be invited to play a small role in her wedding. I will never forget the pre-wedding dinner we all shared together. It was lighthearted and fun, with enough years of college behind us to make us feel grown. I laughed a lot with her that night and we shared a sweet moment just before she was married. She called me E and I called her B, and I looked in her eyes and told her I was so happy for her. She was glowing, as she often seemed to be.

I prayed for her a lot on her wedding day. She was the first of our friends to be married, not even twenty-one. I watched her walk down the aisle in that pretty white dress, her blonde hair swooped up just like the brides in the magazines. I imagined her future, her children, and considered the mystery and covenant of marriage.

Two weeks later, in the middle of June, I was outside reading on the deck at my parents' house when I got the call. The moments that define our life seem to show up in the middle of the most ordinary days. It was Summer, one of the Great Eight, who I had known since childhood. As soon as I heard her voice, I knew something was wrong. She sounded hesitant, distant, and unfamiliar. I could feel the room disappear around me, and my heart doubled up as if to brace my body for the news I somehow knew was coming.

There had been an accident.

Brandy and her husband came home from their honeymoon and were on their way to meet their family at the beach. Her husband was ahead of her in a separate car. Her car crossed the yellow line and she died on impact. I attended her funeral in the same church where she had been married only weeks before. She was buried in her wedding gown.

It sounds too small to say it was devastating to have to say goodbye to her. There was no denying the pain, the fear, or the anxiety that followed me around in the days after her funeral. The idea of seeking closure after losing her was offensive at best. I'm not sure closure is possible when you lose someone you love. But something I learned in the midst of that heartache is that Jesus is present when people are broken.

In the midst of great need, in the midst of a situation where he could not find rest for himself, the psalmist recognized he needed someone to stand up for him. "Who will rise up for me against the evildoers? . . . Unless the LORD had been my help, my soul would soon have settled in silence. If I say, 'My foot slips,' Your mercy, O LORD, will hold me up. In the multitude of my anxieties within me, Your comforts delight my soul" (Ps. 94:16–19 NKJV). He did not ask, "How is it that I am to stand up against this?" Rather, he knew he could not and cried out for someone to stand in his place.

I need a healer, someone to stand on my behalf against my past, against the pain and disappointments of broken relationships, against any fear of trusting in the future, against the sorrow and anger of death. Hiding doesn't work. Running doesn't work. And pretending to be strong only works for a time. We don't need fixing. We need healing. We need someone to take the arrows the enemy has aimed at the deep places of our souls. Someone to stand up when we're falling down. Someone to heal.

Beautifully Broken

Our church has been walking through a series on brokenness titled "Beautifully Broken." What at first glance seems to be an oxymoron is turning out to be an accurate description of the road to freedom. Freedom from the illusion of control. Freedom from the need to be right all the time. Freedom from the fears of serious things, like death and dying, and of irrational things, like believing that a perfectly organized house will bring peace.

It isn't natural to stay broken. I want to shake it better. I want to take it back to the store. That's the do-it-yourself option, the one where I stay strong and put on a good front and think I can handle things. It's the one where I try to avoid the messy at any cost. It's the all-about-me option.

And it doesn't work. Turns out, there is another option. One called trust. And I learn what it is to fall to the ground like a seed, allowing the shell of my self-life to break apart so that the Healer's life can burst forth.

⌒ஒ BEHIND THE MASK ஒ⌒

There is a difference between closure and healing. In the midst of your broken places, are you searching for a mask, for closure, for control? Or are you desperate for a healer?

Jesus will bring us to the edge of self-sufficiency, an uncomfortable place where we have to choose what we will believe. This choice often feels like death: "Unless a grain of wheat falls into the earth and dies, it remains alone . . ." There may be fear in the dying to those masks we wear, in the letting go of the false securities we have built up and stood upon for so long. But God, through Jesus, has overcome every kind of death, and he promises that "if it dies, it bears much fruit" (John 12:24). What is the fruit that comes from falling to the ground?

16

safe, even in failure

For when I am weak, then I am strong.
—2 Corinthians 12:10

One of the good girl's most basic fears is failure. Whether it is in relationships, in our homes, in the workplace, or in the kitchen, good girls tend to avoid those things where failure is a possibility.

There are different types of failure. The first isn't necessarily a sin-type of failure. Rather, this is when we fail to live up to some expectation we have of the way things ought to be. Sometimes it may be legitimate, like setting a goal at work and not meeting it, or trying out a new recipe and ending up with take-out. Other times this commonplace failure feels epic but is merely perceived.

For example, when I hear women tell their childbirth stories, my tendency in my flesh is to tune out. Part of that is because there is an invisible competition between women regarding the process of birth. The length of labor, the number of pushes, the use or non-use of drugs, the weight of the baby—it is all so comparative. But here is the other reason: I have had two C-sections. And I still battle feelings of failure because of it.

When I tell people that, they look at me funny, like I have something on my face. And in a way, I do. It's called the mask of strength and responsibility. And it is falling apart.

I've heard friends of mine who have struggled through infertility say similar things, as if they are somehow less female because their bodies refuse to get pregnant. I have felt less-than because I had to have C-sections, as if maybe I couldn't handle natural childbirth or I haven't passed the test of motherhood without this rite of passage. After my friends have babies, their husbands almost always say things like:

"She is amazing."
"She is the strongest person I've ever known."
"I didn't know she had that in her."
"I am so amazed by her."

And so when my friends have babies, I feel the loss of what I didn't have. I wanted to have my husband think those things of me. I want to be sure people don't think I'm weak, and in my twisted mind I believe natural childbirth would have been proof of it.

So I find myself trying to work in the fact that I endured six hours of labor with the twins before I got an epidural. Or that all my babies were breech and premature so I really didn't have a choice. Or that C-section recovery is super tough. But all that adds up to is me spinning my wheels in order to try to find fleeting worth.

Are these things truly failure? Well, no. But do I have to deal with them as if they were? I think yes. Because the thing about this type of failure, whether real or perceived, is that it reminds me of my own limits and it takes me to a place of recognizing I can't make this life work the way I want, no matter how noble or worthy or good my intentions.

When Good Girls Do Bad Things

Sometimes failure is simply my inability to measure up to an expectation, like having an emergency C-section instead of my preferred method of childbirth. Other times, failure is sin. Though my good-girl story is not laced with controversy or drama, that is not necessarily the way of all good girls. In fact, I know of many women who grew up in the church and were able to maintain a respectable reputation, but they were hiding something very dark and secretive.

Rather than having a general, vague feeling that they aren't good enough, these women have specific things they are aware of where they fall short. Some of these women have struggled with eating disorders or have had abortions or affairs. Some of these girls have considered or even attempted suicide. Some are fighting their way through alcoholism or other types of addiction.

These women are believers. These women are on a journey of discovery. Maybe these women are you. When good girls do bad things, we tend to question their Jesus status. We say that women who really know him couldn't behave in such blatantly unbelieving ways. But the truth is, sometimes they do.

Jane's Story

Jane grew up going to church and loving it. She has sweet memories of Sunday school and truly enjoyed her early childhood years. But late one summer just before entering middle school, things began to change. Her parents suddenly split, leaving Jane wondering how this could have happened in her family when she never even knew her parents were having problems. Things were not as they should be.

Eventually her mom remarried, and Jane was moved away from everything familiar: her school, her family, her father, and her home. They continued attending church where she learned rules and doctrine, but at home she watched as the

grown-ups in her life made decisions that seemed to contradict what they said they believed. The faith and support that
parents are meant to offer was absent for Jane, and whether
they intended it or not, she experienced a sense of rejection
because of it. She began to believe that because she came
from a broken family, she was therefore broken herself. Her
parents didn't seem to expect things to go well for her, and
she began to believe them.

Jane was a good girl with a tender conscience. She was shy,
painfully so. She felt insecure just at the time when security
means so much—on the cusp of puberty. To her, purity and
salvation were closely connected, and it seemed that her mom
and stepdad liked it this way, as it kept her in line. As a young
teenager, Jane followed the rules because of fear of what
might happen if she broke them. She desperately wanted to
grow up, find a man who had waited for her the way she was
waiting for him, get married, have children, and belong to a
church. And even though Jesus often felt more like a burden
than a savior, she still had good intentions and hopes that
if she continued to delight herself in him, he would give her
the desires of her heart (Ps. 37:4). And she held on to those
desires for a long time.

Jane finished high school and went on to a prestigious
college with a major that guaranteed success and a lucrative
career. If there was one thing her parents taught her it was
that she needed a contingency plan, because her desire for
marriage would probably not pan out. Anticipate rejection.
Plan for the worst. Depend on yourself. And by all means,
be a good girl.

By the time Jane was finished with college and living on
her own, there was still no man in sight for her. That verse she
had held on to for so long about God giving her the desires
of her heart began to mock rather than encourage. *Maybe
God is so busy giving all those other girls the desires of their
hearts that he has forgotten me.* So as a twenty-something
good girl, Jane decided it was time to meet her own needs.

She met a respected, impressive businessman who didn't know the Lord but seemed to notice her. He did not sweep her off her feet, but she had long since given up believing that would happen anyway. In the course of their relationship, it quickly became apparent that Jane was a virgin and just as apparent that he was not. But she was a grown-up now, and she had logged her time of waiting. She desperately, *desperately* wanted to ease the pain of her singleness. She longed to be loved. And so she gave in, hoping it would lead to marriage. Unfortunately, it didn't.

Now she saw herself not only as damaged goods but as completely and utterly alone. She spent the next few years floundering, struggling through the tangled mess of her tarnished reputation in the eyes of the people in her church, while at the same time desperately wishing she could find a place to fit in there. She was falling behind in the game of life, watching as her peers from high school were settling down with spouses and babies and respected roles in the church. As a single woman, she felt quarantined in the singles ministry, unimportant and unseen.

Every Sunday was the same routine. She would walk down the carpeted stairs of her small condo, make a pot of coffee, and open the paper to the Celebrations section to see how many people had been married the day before. *There's one more good man who is unavailable to me.* She would drink down that bitter cup, dress for church, and walk in to "worship the Lord." And that was her life for years.

It seemed to Jane that her biggest fears had all come true. She was living her contingency plan. She had been rejected. She was alone.

While at a conference in Texas for church and ministry leaders, I attended a workshop led by Presten Gillham, author of *Grace in Ungracious Places*. During the workshop, he spoke of God's pervasive, never-ending, overwhelming grace.

He described a persistent misconception in our view of God when we find ourselves out in the middle of failures and bad decisions. We turn around and see a faraway God, hands on hips, staring at us. And we believe we have to make our way across all the ungracious territory that we have just traveled through in order to get to him. And then we wonder why we drag our feet getting there. It is impossible to retrace those steps. *What if I can't re-create the mess to get back to God?*

These words of Presten's have stayed with me for the past ten years: "Worry and fear are simply the belief that I have gotten myself into a place where God is not. And so that brings us to the truth, that God, through his determination to share his heart with me, was willing to go to my ungracious place to be with me. He would rather die than live without me, even if it means ungracious places."[1]

As hard as it is for this good girl to believe, failure is not the ultimate disqualifier. There has never existed an unredeemable failure. Jane eventually learned this for herself. She met Matt in the midst of her faith struggle, in the midst of her fears that perhaps God wasn't there for her after all. She had not gotten her act together or her ducks in a row, and her and Matt's relationship was far from perfect. But since they married and began building a life together, their mistakes are being beautifully redeemed in the way they are choosing to raise their children.

Jane admits, "It took growing up and experiencing answers to prayers in tangible ways to see that God hadn't forgotten about me. That, along with being in environments where I was able to hear other women share their stories and learn that I wasn't the only one whose life wasn't tied up in a neat little bow."

It is so important to share our weaknesses, failures, and regrets with other women we trust. In those honest environments, Jane was able to receive healing and relief from her painful past.

Jane learned that God doesn't always give the *immediate* desires of our hearts. That isn't what the verse means, anyway. Looking back, she acknowledges, "God knew the deepest

desires, the ones I had given up on, the ones we're too embarrassed to admit to anyone, even ourselves, for fear of being
ridiculed because of them. Those are the desires he's in the business of fulfilling, and he redeems our mistakes for his glory."

If you want biblical proof of the relentless love Jesus has
for us when we fail, you need look no further than Peter.

Peter's Story

As one of the twelve disciples, Peter was someone whom Jesus
was closer to than most others. Peter saw the miracles with
his own eyes and touched those who were healed with his own
hands. Peter walked with Jesus, ate with Jesus, prayed with
Jesus. He should have been more than convinced. Sometimes
it doesn't matter what our eyes have seen. The voice of fear
can be powerfully persuasive.

I don't think Peter's intention was to deny that he was a
disciple of Jesus. It just . . . happened. His impulses were
overwhelming, kind of like that day in the garden when he
drew his sword and cut off the ear of the high priest's slave.
Peter was not known for thinking before he acted. So when
the slave girl asked him if he was one of Jesus' disciples, his
response may have even surprised him: "I am not."

His first denial of Jesus may have come unwittingly, but
by the third time Peter was painfully aware of what he had
done. Especially when he heard that rooster crow.

In that moment, Peter's eyes met those of his Creator as
the Lord turned and looked directly at him. The prophetic
words rushed back in a wild current of regret: *The rooster
will not crow until you deny me three times.* The statement
swirled heavy in his mind, his heart broken and ashamed.
As the bitter tears fell, he knew exactly what he had done.
He may have denied Jesus, but he couldn't deny the fact that
he had failed.

This is not the rebellious failure of a nonbeliever. This is
a person in Jesus' most sacred, hand-picked inner circle. He

was a disciple, a believer, a good guy, and a friend. Peter was in a dark, unwelcoming, ungracious place. Jesus was crucified before Peter had any chance to reconcile. There was no chance for apology, no opportunity to right the wrong, no space for explanation.

So what did Peter do? He went fishing.

For three years Peter was with Jesus. During that time, there is much evidence to suggest that, even though Peter was walking with the Lord, his confidence rested in himself. But that illusion of control was shattered the day he recognized his own failure. The only thing he knew to do was to go back to where he had been before he ever met Jesus. Isn't that what we do when we feel as though we've failed beyond redemption? It comes as no surprise that when Peter and the other disciples went out that night, they caught nothing. Once you have tasted the new, going back to the old will never satisfy.

In a picture of new morning mercies, there appeared a far-away shadow of hope. "But when the day was now breaking, Jesus stood on the beach" (John 21:4). The should-be-dead man stood strong and tall on that beach in the morning light. He called them *children* and asked if they had fish, then told them to cast their net on the right-hand side of the boat. The net quickly filled up with too many fish to lift. In that moment, John turned to Peter and said, "It is the Lord." And Simon Peter, the disciple who failed in the worst way imaginable, threw himself into the sea to get to the risen Jesus.

Consider what most parents would do after their child has failed. They may ask why. They may lecture. They may say something like, "You have broken our trust and now you need to earn it back." In fact, in my flesh, that is precisely what I want to do myself when I fail. *I'll show you how trustworthy I am! I'll prove to you that I will never fail again!* But this is not what Jesus asks of Peter.

Instead, he asks if Peter loves him. *That can't be right,* I think. *Who can speak of love in the wake of such horrible failure? What does love matter?* My flesh calls for action, for

189

payment, for worthiness. But the Spirit of the living, overcoming Jesus invites Peter to love. He does not ask Peter why or tell him to earn anything. In fact, he gives him an even bigger assignment than before: *If you love me, tend my sheep.* Take care of the believers. Disciple my followers. Lead them, love them, care for them, be my hands and feet on earth.

My pastor, Don Miller, recently shared the story of Peter and spoke of the beautiful truth of redemption, encouraging us to believe that no failure is beyond Jesus' reach. "Your failure does not define you," he said. "In Christ, your failure can *redefine* you." Peter initially gave in to temptation and went back to fishing because that's what was familiar. But Jesus came and found him as he hid in that boat on the sea. He found him and he called him to a greater task on one condition: Peter had to be exclusively devoted to Christ. Fear could no longer drive him. Love had to prevail.

The Owing

Speaking of love after such an offense is baffling when I consider it from behind my mask. It seems to me that Peter's failure warranted a great deal from Jesus, and none of it had to do with love. It seems to me that hurt and anger would have been legitimate responses. Didn't Jesus have a right to be angry, sad, bitter, and hurt? Peter wouldn't have blamed him. He would have expected it. Instead, Peter not only had to confront his own failure but he had to receive genuine forgiveness for it.

My fear of, regret over, and inability to handle failure has kept me in hiding. But it isn't only my failure that keeps me from living free. I hold myself to an impossible standard, *but I hold you to it too.* And I hold him to it and her to it and them to it. No one is exempt. Sometimes it seems justified, this unwillingness to let go of others' failures. His failure affects me, hurts me, and cuts me deep. Her failure offends me, insults me, and disregards me. The failures of our parents,

190

spouses, friends, and co-workers are especially offensive to good girls. It's why the prodigal son story is so difficult for us. Because not only have I been wronged when you fail, but the expectation that I have to forgive you flies in the face of everything I have worked for. I cannot set you free, because that is too easy for you. If you receive my forgiveness, then you no longer owe me anything. I like to be owed. Your owing me creates a false security for me, one I'm not willing to let go of. So I hold on to my right to be right, to be mad, and to be good.

And in so doing, I live what I actually believe: you should pay for your own sin at your expense and to my benefit, and I get to say when you've paid a high enough price. And oh, by the way, my forgiveness is really expensive. It might cost you everything. And if you aren't willing to give up everything for me, then maybe you don't really love me.

The Rights

Refusing to forgive is ugly. In fact, it could be the number one thing that keeps people from living free. But understand that the reason it is so difficult to extend forgiveness to those who have failed us is because *we are unable to receive forgiveness for our own failures*. We believe we have to work hard to make God smile, to earn his favor, to keep him happy. We believe our mistakes discredit, our failures disqualify, and our lack proves our worthlessness. When what you do determines who you are, then failure *to do* means failure *to be*. The only antidote to the poisonous lie of performance is forgiveness. We have to receive forgiveness in order to live free because we cannot give what we have not first received.

It is easy to move through life unaware of the rights we hold so possessively. The right to be right. The right to be angry. The right to hold on to my hurt. We rehearse hurtful situations in our heads and repeat them to sympathetic friends and any other willing listeners. Or if our hiding is so extreme

191

that it keeps us from speaking our hurt out loud, then we rehearse it to ourselves and let it fester deep into our hearts.

Our masks complicate this process because we know it isn't good to hold on to unforgiveness. So we hide behind our mask of indifference or we get busy in our performance to hide the hurt, the anger, and the pain that has been inflicted upon us. It is a toxic, exhausting way to live. It is not the way of Jesus.

To admit that the offense hurts is necessary to our healing. To feel the pain caused by the failure of others is honest and human and okay. I do not know the extent to which someone else has hurt you. I do not know how deeply their failure has affected you. But I do know this: you will never be more free than when you let go of your right to be the good one.

Imagine a scenario where you are 100 percent right and they are 100 percent wrong. Have you been legitimately hurt? Yes. Is the other person wrong? Yes. Have they asked you for your forgiveness? Maybe. Maybe not. Do they know they have hurt you so much? I don't know. Which is more important to you: to be right or to be free?

Please understand what I am saying. I am *not* saying we are to forget the pain caused by the sin of those around us. I am *not* saying we are to be doormats. I *am* saying we are to depend on Jesus, period. You don't have to protect yourself. If you continue to put your own insatiable desire to be right and heard and understood as the central hub on the wheel of your life, you will forever be going nowhere, and you may never be free.

The Gain in Release

I can't think of a better place to discover where we are hiding than when we are faced with failure—both our own and others'. If you are still hiding behind your mask, then you will be unable to let go of your own failure and you will be unable to forgive the failure of others. But if your life is hidden with Christ in God, then failure loses the power it used to have over you.

Something that keeps us from falling to the ground like a seed is the fact that there are so many things we believe we are entitled to. We hold a fistful of hopes and dreams and desires and wants. I don't mean material things, although that is certainly possible. But those things are easier to recognize. Rather, it is the stuff of good girls, the things we believe are owed to us.

> Brokenness is evident when you no longer react with your previous flesh patterns [masks] when the following rights are challenged:
>   Your right to a good reputation.
>   Your right to have acceptance.
>   Your right to be successful.
>   Your right to have pleasant circumstances.
>   Your right to beauty or strength.
>   Your right to have friends.
>   Your right to be heard.
>   Your right to take offense.
>   Your right to avoid reaping what you sow.
>   Your right to be right.
>   Your right to see results.
>   Your right to be loved by others.[2]

It has helped me to literally make a list of all of the things I either think or wish I had control over, and then to offer them to Jesus, honestly and out loud. There is power in hearing my own voice speak those things I so tightly hold on to, because these rights are the breeding ground for my masks. They are like seeds planted in the soil of my soul. If I continue to care for them and feed them and give them time to grow, then their roots travel deep and their blooms show up in the form of a do-good mask.

Jesus Christ was God on earth. But he was also fully, completely, literally man. If anyone had rights to claim, it was him. But he didn't. Instead, Paul tells us, "Your attitude should be the same as that of Christ Jesus: Who, being in very nature God, did not consider equality with God something to be grasped, but made himself nothing, taking the very nature of a servant, being made in human likeness. And being found in appearance as a man, he humbled himself and became obedient to death—even death on a cross!" (Phil. 2:5–8 NIV).

The phrase *something to be grasped* literally means "something to seize and hold." It is the Greek noun *harpagmos* that comes from the root word *harpazō*, or to commit robbery.[3] In other words, his equality with God was not considered to be robbery, because he is, in his very nature, God. But he emptied himself of those God-rights on earth, letting them go so completely that they were no longer recognizable as his. He chose instead the life of a dependent servant, trusting his Father for everything. He released all rights in order to come to earth. He was both the Creator of life as well as the most dependent man who ever lived.

A Common Frailty

Living as a good girl, there are times when I've seen the value of my life as only equal to the sum of my failures. There can be a false humility that comes from that dark place. *I'm a failure and I'm good for nothing.* And then, it can flip on a dime when someone sins against me. *They have failed and they should pay. How could they do that to me?* I move quickly from false humble to puffed-up pride. Back and forth, day to day. Jesus is the only One who can step in and stop that pendulum swinging. He offers a new definition of humble—seeing yourself as God sees you. No more and no less.

In the same way your failure doesn't define you, *their* failure doesn't define you, either. It may be true that your husband committed adultery, but his sin does not therefore mean you are worthless. It may be true that your friend carelessly disregarded your feelings and opinions, but her disregard does not therefore mean you don't matter. It may be true that your mother abandoned you as a child, but her sin does not therefore mean you are unlovable. They may have hurt you, but don't let them define you. Because the truth is, Jesus came to stand between you and that hurt.

There is no immunity to the frailty of this humanity, as much as I wish there were. Life is so much further from my control than even I know. This earthy, fleshy, eyes down perspective I live with keeps me living a small story. We cannot release these rights on our own. Without Christ, these rights are all we have. But with him, we can release the right to be perfect and never mess up. We can release the right to pay for our own failure. And we can release those around us from having to pay for their failures as well. As we surrender to Christ's power (knowing he is bigger than I am) and to his love (knowing he has my best interests in mind), we are able to experience strength from weakness, beauty from ashes, and freedom even in the midst of failure.

BEHIND THE MASK

Can you identify any areas in your life where you have experienced failure that isn't sin? Perhaps you had an expectation of yourself that you were unable to reach or a desire to accomplish something in which you fell short. How did you reconcile this type of failure with the masks you wear?

Can you identify any areas in your life where you have experienced failure that is sin? Perhaps you can relate with Jane's story, or maybe you have experienced deep regret in other ways. How has that type of failure influenced the way you relate to God?

195

Until we consciously release the rights we hold on to, it may be impossible for us to receive and extend forgiveness. Some of my own personal rights I've had to continue to release: my right to meet every need of my husband, my right to never disappoint people, my right to a clean and organized house, my right to be able to explain myself, my right to be the favorite. What are some of the rights you hold tightly in your hand? Are you willing to release them in exchange for Jesus?

17

·················

safe, even when it all goes wrong

You are my safe and secret place; you will keep me from trouble; you will put songs of salvation on the lips of those who are around me.

—Psalm 32:7 BBE

*W*hen Heather found out she was pregnant in the fall of 2000, she knew there could be complications. She gave birth to a son only five months prior, and that had been a difficult pregnancy. For the most part, though, her second pregnancy moved along smoothly, with only the typical fatigue and morning sickness. When she and her husband moved to a new city during her nineteenth week, she was told that because of her previous high-risk pregnancy she would need to consult a perinatologist before being accepted by an obstetrician.

Sitting in the waiting room at the specialist's office, Heather considered this visit to be a formality, a necessary step before meeting her regular OB. She saw many pregnant women sitting around her and silently wondered what was wrong with their babies. She was thankful that her baby was healthy and well, a thought that would haunt her by day's end.

The nurse called her back into the examining room, and she entered into lighthearted chitchat with the ultrasound technician about baby names and the due date—normal pregnant things. After only a few minutes, the air shifted in the room, and the technician grew tense and quiet. Something was clearly wrong.

"Mrs. George, I am so very sorry." They are the words you don't want to hear during an ultrasound, words that bring fear to life. The ultrasound revealed that Heather's baby girl had an enlarged heart. It was a condition that could not be repaired. The baby was experiencing the final stages of heart failure and would die before her due date.

Babies are not supposed to die before their due date. Mothers are not supposed to have to cope with the fatal diagnosis of their children. Things were going wrong. Very wrong.

Fear barreled down on top of Heather, speeding out of control. Like a heavy, dark smoke, the fear swirled around her with questions and worry-guilt: *Could I have stopped this? I had the flu a few months back and didn't go to the doctor. Is this my fault?*

There she sat, surrounded by specialists with medical degrees and years of experience, in a room filled with medicines and instruments that were supposed to make people healthy and well. And the only thing those professionals could tell her was to call when the baby stopped kicking.

Those doctors were only people. The hospital was just a building. So Heather and her husband planned a funeral for their baby. She readied herself to give birth to a baby who had already died. She cried uncontrollably for days. They picked out a casket.

Unexpected Peace

The day they were scheduled to pick out their baby girl's nameplate, Heather woke up with an unexplainable peace. She was determined this baby was not going to die and wanted to get a second opinion. Knowing that a main stage of grief was denial, her husband lovingly supported her and they found another doctor to consult. To their great surprise, this doctor disagreed with the first diagnosis, encouraging them to carry the baby to thirty-four weeks in order to treat her outside the womb. In the midst of questions (*Why didn't we do this sooner?*), there was also the most vague sense of hope. But it was not a joyful hope. Heather describes that time as "anticipation without excitement; longing without joy. Fear."

Heather continued to carry the baby until her own health required an emergency C-section. "I remember the nurse asking us if we wanted to sign DNR papers, and again we declined. It was awkward because you could tell the staff didn't know how to act. Some were acting like it was a normal delivery, while others couldn't help but check on me and rub my arms every time they walked by. I just wanted it over. I wanted to face what was coming and move on with life. This had taken away a part of me that I don't think I will ever get back. Innocence was lost. We had been told she wouldn't cry when she was born, and we had prepared for our first meeting with her to be heart wrenching. We hadn't really prepared for what actually happened." The baby not only cried, she wailed. Congratulations were tossed around, and the surgeon handed her off to the NICU team. They named her Emma, meaning "whole."

She continued to breathe for five months with the help of a ventilator. During that time, they waited for a heart for their little girl. The day they got the call, Heather prepared herself for the worst while longing for a new beginning. She grieved for the donor family who lost their baby, while also rejoicing in the hope for her own. The surgery went well, and two weeks later they were allowed to take their baby girl home.

What they thought was the end of this most difficult journey was only the beginning of another. Though she had received her heart well, Emma was not gaining any weight or able to sit up. By now she was ten months old. Heather researched online, spoke with other mothers who had babies with similar symptoms, and eventually got in contact with a specialist. In her frantic search for answers, she never stopped to consider what the answers might reveal. After more tests and analysis, it was discovered that the baby's diagnosis was terminal. Not only that, if the doctors had properly diagnosed her in the beginning, she never would have been eligible for a transplant.

Remarkably, Emma continued to fight over the next five years. Heather and her husband worked hard to find a doctor who was qualified and willing to treat their daughter, who was also diagnosed with autism. They found a doctor, and in the process they discovered Emma's new heart was failing her too. She would need another transplant.

That was January of 2006. She is still waiting.[1]

One year later, after struggling with a virus that caused damage to her inner ear, Heather visited her ear, nose, and throat specialist. While there, the doctors found a large tumor in her brain. At first Heather was told it was inoperable, but after a second (and third) opinion, she discovered otherwise and was immediately scheduled for surgery. They removed the tumor and began radiation and chemotherapy.[2]

I met Heather a few years after that treatment. You don't realize what a difference hair makes until it isn't there. When I met her, I assumed she had been through a lot. I assumed it all had to do with her cancer. I could never have guessed about her daughter's struggles as well. It's almost as if all the things she had been through with Emma prepared her for the cancer.

"It isn't about the cancer, it isn't about what it has the ability to do to our bodies, it isn't about the treatments or the part of us it takes away; it's about the journey. It's about rediscovering the parts of yourself that you never ever knew or dreamed existed, and giving them room to grow and room to take flight. It's about seeing life through cancer's eyes and being better because of it, being more whole and more alive despite it. It's about living."

Even though the first thing I noticed about Heather was her bald head, that most certainly was not my final impression of her. When I think of this brave woman, I think instead of these words she spoke that bring me great comfort when I begin to fear the unknown future: "I do not fear what my future holds. I can't. I can't spend the energy anticipating the next horrible event. I am choosing to anticipate the next great provision, whatever provision that may be. I am choosing to believe that no matter what, even if God calls me home tonight in my sleep, He never stepped off His throne. He simply brought me closer to it."[3]

Permission to Feel the Pain

Heather will be the first person to admit the anger, the fear, and the fist shaking that went on with God about her daughter's sickness and her own brain tumor. But she did not stay in that place. Heather knew she was safe in the presence of her Father. When faced with death, safe takes on an entirely new meaning. If anyone knows what it is like when it all goes wrong, Heather knows. But she also knows that she is safe.

She could have chosen to believe God was ignoring her. Instead she chose love, to believe she was loved, and to love in return.

It is tempting to think, *Well, if someone like Heather can make it through a child's terminal illness, an autism diagnosis, and a brain tumor, then why can't I make it 'til lunch?* Sometimes I hear stories like Heather's and think *Wow. Look at what she's been through. Now you don't have it so bad, do you?* But the truth is, every heart knows its own pain. My dear friend Holley writes about feeling guilty for struggling when it seemed other people had it so much worse, until the words of a wise college professor came to mind: "Do not compare your pain with others. The worst pain you will ever feel is

201

your own. That does not mean you are selfish—that means you are human."[4] I don't tell Heather's story to make you feel guilty. I tell it because the faith it takes for her to make it through a brain tumor is the same faith it takes me to make it 'til lunch. It's all Jesus. It's all dependence. Sometimes it's just harder to see our need when we are healthy and well.

My Own Pain

When John and I decided we wanted to have a baby, I think I believed the hard part would be deciding when we were ready. I did not expect to have to wait. Month after month, I was whipped around in the last car of my emotional roller coaster, wishing for two pink lines and always seeing only one. It felt so impossibly hopeless, the waiting and not knowing, looking for signs, hoping against hope, taking negative test after negative test. I had really long cycles, so while most women could find out on day 35 or 36 if they were pregnant, I would be still waiting on day 60, with no period and no positive test. It was maddening to want something so badly but have absolutely zero control over getting it.

It was not a brain tumor. But it was my own pain. I knew the Lord was calling me to trust, but I didn't want to hear it. Because to me, trusting him meant *I'm not pregnant.* So I looked to books, to the internet, to friends and family members who had children, trying to find hope and assurance, some glimmer of truth or confirmation that I could be pregnant. I would calculate fake due dates based on made-up conception dates, and hope and wish and plan that one of them would come to be. None of that satisfied, because when the conversation ended, when the article was read, when the tears paused, the truth remained that I simply didn't know.

So I asked the Lord what he thought about all this, and this is what he said to me: *I am the Lord your God. I am your refuge and strength, an ever-present help in trouble* (see Ps.

202

46:1). I sensed him there with me, quietly, patiently, lovingly there. He waited until my questions were finished. He waited until I really wanted to know his answers to those questions. Perhaps he waited for me to ask the right question. And I held on to that hope and encouragement for about a week until I was once again powerfully confronted with the same fear, worry, and hopelessness.

In his book *The Pressure's Off*, Dr. Larry Crabb shares a story about this process of trust and defeat. A friend of his was living in the midst of difficult, hopeless days. They spent the morning together to pray and talk through how the Spirit was working within him. By lunchtime, his friend's outlook had entirely changed, though his circumstances were decidedly unchanged: "I'm deeply confident God is blessing me with the chance to know Him as I never have before. And it's happening. I've never felt so confident in His goodness, and somehow that confidence and my trials have made me not care as much what people think or even whether things turn around, though I wish they would. I'm miserable but I'm content. As I lose hope for things ever getting good, I'm gaining hope in God's doing a good work in me."[5]

And then I am reminded of this verse: "Now to Him who is able to do far more abundantly beyond all that we ask or think, according to the power that works within us, to Him be the glory in the church and in Christ Jesus to all generations forever and ever. Amen" (Eph. 3:20–21). Things go wrong. And when they do, he is with us in them. He is for us. He is in us.

Four months after that conversation with Jesus, I discovered I was pregnant with twins. Far more abundantly beyond, indeed.

It doesn't always work out so beautifully. That's why it is so important to cherish those times when it does, so that the track record of faithfulness the Lord is building into our lives will mean something during the times when things go wrong.

Receive the Little

One practical way to set our minds when it all goes wrong is to practice receiving truth in small ways when things go right. Celebrating the small things does not come natural to me. Most of the time I am in survival mode, just thankful to make it to bedtime. But before we can cling to truth when it all goes wrong, it's necessary to receive those daily graces as gifts when things are going well.

God invites us to receive by offering small gifts on a daily basis as evidence of his presence and existence. "Every good thing given and every perfect gift is from above, coming down from the Father of lights, with whom there is no variation or shifting shadow" (James 1:17). Over the past few years, I have been developing the practice of receiving small gifts as from his hand, including the lovely, the messy, and the unexpected.

The Lovely

As we practice receiving the lovely things as from God's hand, we are perhaps more quick to trust him even when it all goes wrong. What began as an experiment of living in the moment slowly evolved into a habit of seeing on purpose. I'm becoming an intentional noticer and it is leading me into thankfulness for things beyond the obvious. For the mess as well as the masterpiece. For the unexpected as well as the best-laid plans.

Small gifts wait in quiet places. They hide under piles of daily tasks, waiting to be discovered and celebrated. That's why I think Jesus taught us to pray for our daily bread—not bread to last a lifetime, but bread to last this day. It was a call to dependence, a call away from self-sufficiency, a call to turn to the Giver, a call to humbly and thankfully receive.

I romanticize the past, longing for its fuzzy memories to rematerialize so I can hold them in my arms again. I wish for the future to hurry up, certain that in its arrival will be peace and promise and finally, rest. This is the day that the Lord has made, yet I long for another. To find the lovely in the ordinary sometimes takes a bit of work, but the more I look for it, the more quickly it shows up.

The Messy

I had a new friend come over this morning. She's the best kind of new friend. She brought me a really large coffee. From Starbucks. And cinnamon rolls. She is a mom as well, but her kids are in middle school. She asked me a question, and I found myself excited to answer her because it was a real question that required real, cohesive thought. I began to share from my heart about things I have learned and am still learning. I was profound and smart and vulnerable, but for some reason she was not nodding thoughtfully. Rather, she was smiling, almost laughing. Why, you ask?

Turns out she was distracted by my pacing from one needy child to the next. As I talked, evidently I also pried open one mouth, pulled one baby from the dining room table (four times), settled three arguments, dressed two Polly Pockets, and took 147 steps while pacing the floor. I didn't even realize it until she opened her mouth and said these beautiful words: "There's a reason why the laundry doesn't get done."

It was nice for someone who's been there to recognize that which I already know: I can work hard all day and still get nothing done. The only proof that I worked at all is my sore back, tired feet, and, of course, the piles and piles of laundry.

At 8:30 p.m. it feels like midnight. Blinking takes effort. I'm tightly clenching my jaw as I type, and I. Can't. Stop. This life is exhausting. And I'm not even sick or pregnant or depressed or dying of starvation or homeless. But I still need a hero. Good thing I've got one. I can receive the mess as a gift because it gives me the opportunity to tell God, "I've thrown myself headlong into your arms—I'm celebrating your rescue" (Ps. 13:5 Message). How life-giving it is to know I have someplace else to throw myself headlong other than into my bed. Besides, it isn't made and the sheets are dirty.

The Unexpected

To receive the daily interruptions as from the hand of God is probably the most difficult for me. I went to bed on a Sunday night with big plans for the day ahead—finally, a day to write. But a morning thermometer with a reading of 101.3 set all those plans high up on the shelf.

My girl needed me.

I want to say I put the plans up and left them there, but I didn't. Instead, I tried to reach them all day, pulling up a stool to stand on and putting her off for one more minute. I became snappy, overwhelmed, and un-surrendered. I grasped for a way to resurrect that worn-out day. Maybe there wasn't time to write or think or be silent alone, but if I was able to just finish something, anything: the dishes, the folding, the floors. All the while, there she sat, snuggled up on the couch alone. I was around, even in the room. But I wasn't present.

It wasn't long before shame showed up again—shame for not wanting to just sit with my sick girl, shame for not finishing the dishes, shame for wanting to finish the dishes, and shame for having shame. By the end of the day, I was exhausted with nothing to show for it. I had been battling on the inside, fighting for time, for a change of circumstance, and for completion.

Sarah Young wrote one of my favorite devotional books, titled *Jesus Calling*. In it, she says this: "Enjoy the tempo of a God-breathed life by letting Him set the pace."[6]

My daughter is home sick with a fever even though I have a deadline to meet . . . *the tempo of a God-breathed life . . .*

The Check Engine light comes on in my car even though I just had it serviced . . . *the tempo of a God-breathed life . . .*

School is closed for snow, all three kids have strep, and I'm scheduled to leave for a conference in exactly twelve hours . . . *the tempo of a God-breathed life* . . .

A girlfriend with a new baby calls just to chat because she feels crazy and needs a friend even though I have forty-seven errands to run . . . *the tempo of a God-breathed life* . . .

My husband asks me to pray with him but I'm in a really bad mood . . . *the tempo of a God-breathed life* . . .

The doctor calls with bad news . . . *the tempo of a God-breathed life* . . .

As Heather and her family continue to struggle through Emma's health issues, she recently wrote this on her blog: "No matter what today entails, no matter what each moment holds, good things will happen. Good things always happen amidst the bad. You would think by now, with all that I have gone through, I would have learned that. You would think that I would have mastered the art of looking for the positive in all situations. But I haven't. And that is okay. It is okay for me to be angry at this situation. It doesn't mean that I have lost hope. In the midst of the pain and heartbreak that I have felt, I am looking towards the good. I am turning my face to Him and letting those words fall on me like rain."[7]

To accept the lovely, the messy, and the unexpected things in our days, knowing that God sees them and has an eternal perspective, is to say with confidence *I receive your timing. I accept that you know so I don't have to. Even when it all goes wrong.*

⌒ BEHIND THE MASK ⌒

Romans 8:28 says this: "And we know that God causes all things to work together for good to those who love God, to those who are called according to His purpose." Do you believe this statement?

What is the difference between *things going right* and *things working together for good*?

When things go wrong, does it seem to disrupt the tempo of this God-breathed life, or are you able to see those things as part of that tempo?

In what ways have the masks you are used to wearing kept you from enjoying the tempo of a God-breathed life?

18

. . . .

safe, even when you don't feel safe

Begin to believe, and hold on to it steadfastly, that He has taken that which you have surrendered to Him. You positively must not wait to feel either that you have given yourself, or that God has taken you. You must simply believe it, and reckon it to be the case.

—Hannah Whitall Smith,
A Christian's Secret to a Happy Life

Two weeks after John and I returned home from our honeymoon, we joined a few other adults and a group of about twenty-five high school students on a week-long mission trip to Washington, DC. I had never been to the nation's capital, and it was exciting to see all the historic landmarks in person. On the way home as we traveled south down I-95, my friend Jimmy directed everyone to look out the van window. "That's the Pentagon to our right," he said. "Take a good look—it's the most highly secure and protected building in the world."

209

That was in July 2001.

Two months later, the building where people felt the most secure turned out to be a very insecure place. In a horrible, unthinkable act of terrorism, American Airlines Flight 77 crashed into the Pentagon after being hijacked. Everyone on board died as well as over one hundred people in the building. They felt safe, but it turns out they weren't.

Feeling safe does not guarantee safety.

Control

Most days, I conduct my business under the illusion of control. I make decisions about what to have for dinner and where to send my kids to school and how to juggle my time. For the most part, the days pass in a predictable pattern and there is an underlying sense that I have things under control. I feel safe most of the time.

One particular Monday evening, my family and I had just finished a nice dinner together at a restaurant near our house. As we loaded the kids into our car, John teased me about buying coats for looks rather than warmth, and I teased him for having twelve fleece pullovers. We laughed as we entered the busy intersection.

And then another car ran a red light and our safe, warm family car spun out of control.

The illusion was shattered.

A scream escaped without my permission.

Our kids began to cry.

I stared into a smoky nothing, confused as to why the cloudy view through the windshield was of the restaurant we had just left rather than the opposite side of the street where we should have been.

Things were not as they should be.

I heard the familiar sound of my own voice speaking with a calm that didn't reach my heart as I unsuccessfully attempted to convince our girls everything was okay.

210

Later, we watched as our car was towed away, and I considered the vulnerability of humanity. How one moment you are laughing with the love of your life—lighthearted, safe, and normal. And in the midst of those happy sounds, your life is interrupted with an event that is totally beyond your control.

We walked away from that busy intersection with barely a scratch, though our car was totaled beyond repair. I was able to remain calm in the midst of the emergency, but a few hours later as we headed to bed, the anxiety caught up with me, strong and heavy. I lay awake until three in the morning, stricken with worry about what could have been. It was as though my room was filled up with fear and I was taking it in with deep breaths, allowing the dark gray of uncertainty to swirl within me and settle deep inside. The *what-ifs* were haunting, pulling against my attempts to trust. *What if the other car had been going even faster? What if it had been bigger? What if one of my kids . . . ? What if my husband . . . ?*

Was I safe? Yes, I was safe. Was my family safe? Yes, they were safe too. Did I feel safe? No. I felt far from safe. Safe felt like a not-so-funny joke, a faraway reality for other people that would never again be true for me. In the midst of the fear, I sensed the Lord reminding me to rest. I prayed for the anxiety to pass. It didn't. Not for a long time, anyway. So I waited. He waited with me.

He never promises that our families will be safe. Not in the way we think. He does promise his presence, though. And if you don't know him, you may think that is a bad trade-off. There are times when that is how it feels. I want my children. I want my husband. Today I have them all. But control? The idea that I actually have a hand in the way things will go? The veil has been lifted on that illusion.

I am learning more about what it means to have the presence of the Creator of the Universe with me wherever I go. It is important to know I'm not alone, especially in those moments when my life and the lives of those I love are revealed to be vulnerable. Feeling insecure does not always mean you are unsafe, just as feeling safe does not always mean you are safe.

In other words, I can't count on the feelings because they aren't always right. And I may have to redefine what it means to be safe.

My only option is to trust in the One who holds all things together, even when they fall apart. To trust even when it doesn't feel true. To believe in safety even when I don't feel safe. To set my mind on what is true even when it feels foolish and naïve.

One of the hardest times to remember God's truth is in the midst of strong emotion. Fear, worry, or even excitement can cloud our perception of truth. If it doesn't feel true, it's hard to believe it is true.

My Two-Faced Soul

It is so difficult to live contrary to how I feel. That is, until my feelings change. On Monday I feel hopeless to ever plan a good meal with twin babies around, yet on Tuesday I take them both to the grocery store and make a completely enjoyable, healthy meal. I feel fat and ugly on Tuesday night, but strong and full of potential on Wednesday morning. I feel bored and uninspired on Wednesday night, and I plant tulips with a smile on Thursday morning.

My feelings on the soul level will tug and jerk and pull all over. But God is constant, and he put his Spirit within me. My old nature died along with Jesus on the cross, and then he gave me new life in him: "Therefore, if anyone is in Christ, he is a new creation; the old has gone, the new has come!" (2 Cor. 5:17 NIV).

I don't have to live in a state of reacting to whatever my emotions tell me. I can make choices based on the truth and watch as my emotions change. The feelings will eventually change so I can experience the freedom that is mine. As long as I am busy protecting myself, it is difficult for me to experience the life of Christ. As long as I am trapped in the duality of my soul, I will continue to believe the lie that I am what I do, that I cannot act contrary to how I feel. Sometimes I have to take the mask off before I feel safe. I have to risk not knowing and trust that God knows.

When it was time for the Israelites to finally enter the Promised Land, the only thing standing in their way was the Jordan River. God promised Joshua that he would give them every place where they set their feet. The first place their feet were to be set? Right into the waters of the Jordan River. God did not tell them to wait until the waters parted and then walk through on dry ground. The priests were to stand in the river before the waters would part. They would receive the promise, but first they had to get wet.

To Live Free

To experience victory, you absolutely positively cannot wait until you feel safe. Emotions don't have a brain. They are reactors. They may respond to truth, but they may also respond to lies with the same passion and conviction, sometimes more so. You must decide if you will trust the feeling or if you will trust the truth.

In the first nine chapters of this book, we explored the common masks good girls tend to hide behind. In other words, those chapters describe in detail what it looks like when we depend on ourselves to try to make life work instead of depending on Jesus. When your safety is challenged and you recognize that familiar tug to pull out your girl-made mask, ask yourself these four questions instead:

What is the truth? (Spirit)
What will you believe? (Mind)
What will you do? (Will)
Will you give up the right to feel as if God's truth is true? (Emotions)[1]

213

After a long weekend of feeling bad about myself for a five-pound weight gain, I went to a gathering at the home of a friend. Her home was beautiful. The women were also beautiful and stylish, with nice hair and big diamonds. Their jeans fit them just right and their teeth were so very white. It may have been easier to handle if they were rude and snobby like the mean girls in the movies. But they were all so very kind: fun, lovely women with beautiful homes and welcoming hearts.

I sat wilted in that room, surrounded by all that perfection. I felt lazy, ugly, and less-than. Deep inside, I had an urge to run, or to prove ways that I was better even though I felt so much worse. I was a Jesus-loving grown-up, slumped over in a puddle of stretch-mark self-pity. I felt decidedly un-free and un-safe.

In that moment, in the middle of all that mess, I had a fleeting, initially unwelcome thought: *What is the truth here?*

In the midst of wallowing emotions, this question is not one I feel like considering. It takes practice, purpose, and faith. But this question will be the bridge for you between the lie and the truth. If you do not stop to answer this question, you will live in default mode. Your life will be a series of earthly, predictable reactions to people and circumstances. You will either hide behind your mask in fear or rip it off in rebellion, anger, and bitterness at the world you have allowed to spin crazy around you. Instead, remember the questions.

What is the truth? Even though I may feel unsafe and unacceptable, I am accepted in Christ—not because of how much I weigh, but because of how much he loves.

What will you choose to believe? I choose to believe God rather than my feelings. I choose to believe I am acceptable even though I feel unacceptable.

What will you choose to do? I will choose to depend on Christ as my sufficiency and act as an accepted person rather than sit in a corner of self-pity. I will choose to allow God's definition of my acceptance to trump my own.

Will you give up the right to feel as if God's truth is true?
I will choose to continue to depend on Christ even though
I don't yet feel acceptable. I choose to release the right to
manage others' opinions of me and rest in the sufficiency of
the life of Christ.

Don't deny the feelings, but realize it takes no faith to stay
in the feelings. They are like the screen saver that comes up
when the computer is inactive. It is the automatic response,
the natural response. You cannot set your mind on two things
at once. Thoughts may come fast and furious, but they only
come one at a time. Feelings generally follow what our minds
are set on. We get to choose.

Behind all our masks, true safety always seems slightly out
of reach, just beyond the next decision, the next relationship,
the next baby, the next house, the next job. The next. Always
the next.

If I could just stay home with my kids . . .
If I could just go back to work . . .
If I could just get pregnant . . .
If I could just get out of debt . . .
If only I had a college degree . . .
If only I could lose this weight . . .

Jesus is the radical, absolutely complete, living answer to
all our if-onlys and if-I-could-justs. His unwavering, unchang-
ing, unconditional love and acceptance of us is what we are
really looking for.

"For in Him all the fullness of Deity dwells in bodily form,
and in Him *you have been made complete*" (Col. 2:9–10,
emphasis added). When my patience is gone, he offers to
be patience for me. When my strength is spent, he becomes
strength in me. When my faith is small, he believes on my
behalf. Every time.

Recently, I shared some of my own frustrations about the struggles I have between my feelings and my thoughts with my dear friend, mentor, and counselor, Steve Lynam. I loved what he had to say about my feeling self: "As your spirit communes with the Spirit of God, he plants seeds of desire in your heart and then leads you according to his will. And he will work within you such that you will begin to desire what he desires. When you do what would really please you, you are actually obeying God!"

Then, he reminded me of Psalm 23:3 where David says simply, "He restores my soul." As we now know, our soul is our mind, our will, *and* our emotions. He restores all three on my behalf and for his good pleasure. Both our minds and our emotions are in the process of restoration. As we set our minds on truth, our emotions are being renewed as well.

Sometimes when we talk about setting our minds on truth, our feelings and emotions are painted in a negative light. I am still learning what it means to embrace my emotional self and not hide behind my fake fines, while at the same time learning to set my mind on God's truth even when my emotions tell me otherwise. I know God has designed me to feel deeply and fully. Sometimes those emotions lead me in truth and sometimes they don't. I still haven't figured out the perfect balance between those things, but I'm thankful that in Christ, I don't have to. I believe him when he says he is restoring my soul, and I trust him to lead me in the paths of righteousness.

The Truth No Matter What

In this spinning, contradictory, upside-down world, Scripture is the only place to find truth. Sometimes I imagine a world where God's answers to me are personalized, wrapped up in plastic, and delivered to my driveway every morning like the *USA Today*. And I unwrap it while I drink my coffee and soak up my custom-made daily dose of the colored newsprint.

Scripture truth takes effort, digging, and faith. Jesus' truth doesn't come in color, at least not at first. But as I sit with him, as I listen to the words he speaks and let them sink down deep and wide into me, the black and white begins to dance. And like Dorothy opening up the farmhouse door, God's truth paints vibrant, brilliant colors with large, confident strokes on the walls of my soul. His Spirit testifies with my spirit. *Yes! This is true,* they say together. And I begin to practice his truth as *my* truth, regardless of the feelings that fleet and fly.

With the prophet Isaiah, I know that when I walk through the fire, I will not be burned. When I pass through the waters, Jesus will be with me (see Isa. 43:2). Scripture does not say I will not get wet; it says he will be with me. And he is. I need not fear; redemption is true.

Along with the psalmist I can sing of stillness and of knowing that the Lord, he is God (see Ps. 46). God does not say "be still and *feel* like I am God." He says be still, cease striving, make space . . . and *know*. Know it as sure as oxygen and gravity. We have a fortress, a refuge, a safe place. His name is Jesus.

In his name I can do all things, not with strength that comes from visible me, but with impossible strength from invisible him. He does not simply give me strength, he envelops and embodies peacefulness and strength in me and through me and around me.

In Galatians 5, God says through the apostle Paul that the fruit of his Spirit is amazing love, inexpressible joy, overwhelming peace, unending patience, warm kindness, authentic goodness, complete faithfulness, unadulterated gentleness, and Jesus-empowered self-control. I have been given this Spirit. I do not have to work hard, try hard, or make effort to earn this Spirit. As a believer in Jesus Christ—in his death, burial, and resurrection—the truth about Jesus' acceptance before the Father is true about me. He receives me.

John, the disciple whom Jesus loved, tells us that there was a beginning. And in the beginning was the Word, and the

Word was with God and the Word was God (John 1). Jesus is the beginning and the end, and he is indeed the Word. He is the word I need to hear when I need to hear it. He is the One who calms me, comforts me, rejoices over me with love, and delights over me with songs of joy.

Like the sheep in Psalm 23, I may walk through the valley of the shadow of death, but I will fear no evil because he is with me. I will not stop, lie down, or die in that valley. I will walk through and I will not walk through alone. He restores my soul.

Like Paul, I know that I have been crucified with Christ and I—the one who wears the masks and tries to make this dead life work—that me no longer lives, but Christ lives in me. The life I live in this body, I live by faith in the One who loves me and gave himself for me (see Gal. 2:20).

In the end, I don't want to see Jesus fully and in person, look expectantly toward him to finally receive the freedom and rest of my salvation, and hear him say, *Sweet daughter, you have had it all along, but you chose not to believe. You have had abundance, but you have lived in want. I gave you freedom, but you lived in chains. I gave you forgiveness, but you lived with guilt. I gave you completeness, but you hid behind your girl-made masks and pretend identities.*

So let's choose life. Before it's too late, choose life and love and freedom. It is yours for the taking.

Still, doubt creeps in.

This may be true for everyone else, but not for me.
Yes, for you.
It can't be for me.
Even if you were the only one.
It is too good to be true.
Indeed. I am the only good that is true.

God, who is all-knowing, all-powerful, loving, kind, gentle, strong, and forgiving—he lives. And he chooses to live in me.

If I have his resources available to me, if I have God himself available to me, not just to help but to do, then I can indeed bear all things, hope all things, and endure all things.

I can live victoriously in the midst of the dry, arid, hopeless desert in which I sometimes find myself. In that place where water doesn't flow and there is no rest, where it seems his voice can't reach, I am challenged to trust him before I see the river, before I hear songs of love. And so I believe, and then I wait. I first believe the truth is true, and then I wait to feel it.

One of my favorite pictures of safety in Scripture comes from Psalm 139:5–6, where David says, "You have enclosed me behind and before, and laid Your hand upon me. Such knowledge is too wonderful for me; it is too high, I cannot attain to it."

Imagine a day when you are overwhelmed beyond what you thought you could ever bear. Perhaps you just discovered a loved one is sick. Or you have a child who is living contrary to what you know is good for her. Or your husband just lost his job. Maybe you are simply having one of those days where you woke up in a funk. The house is a wreck, the laundry is piled high, the fridge is empty, and it's raining. And you feel fat. Imagine that day. Maybe you don't have to imagine. Maybe you're living that day right now.

Sometimes in those days, it helps to remember that God has enclosed me behind. That means everything in my past—every situation, circumstance, pain, fear, and longing I've ever had—he has been a barrier between those things and me. The Hebrew word translated as "behind" is also used in Scripture to mean "west." And he has also enclosed me before, meaning forward, front, or everlasting. It can also mean "east." East and west are opposites forever. They have no beginning, no ending, and they never meet one another. He covers my yesterday and he holds my tomorrow. Still, this present moment is where I live. What about today?

He has enclosed me forever in the past and forever in the future. And then he lays his hand upon me in the *great right now*. The New Living Translation says it this way: "You go before me and follow me. You place your hand of blessing on my head." Imagine a hero who not only leads the way but also brings up the rear and holds your hand all at the same time. I can't imagine a safer place than that.

The Mask Removal

There is no magic formula to living life free of masks. There is no automatic mask remover. The masks will never disappear completely as long as we live in a fallen world. I have days where it feels as if my only option is to pull out those well-worn masks and move through life in survival mode, content to be good and invisible. But I can't stay there for long, because I have tasted freedom. I know the truth about the rescue; about the way Jesus came into this war-torn world to save me; about the tragic, horrific way he died; about the blood and life he sacrificed so I wouldn't have to. I also know that he didn't stay dead. He rose up again and lives in me this day. And now that actually means something. His Spirit united with my spirit makes every difference. There is nothing I can do to get more of him. I have been given everything I need for life and godliness (2 Pet. 1:3).

Jesus Saves is not just a religious slogan; it is my present-day reality. He saves me from every girl-made inclination I have to make this life work and from the fleshly mask I hide behind when it doesn't. He saves me from my failures as well as my successes. He saves me from the shame of my mistakes as well as the pride of my achievements. He saves me from trying to suck life out of the accolades this world has to offer by placing me safely in him, hidden with Christ in God.

All he asks is that I receive him. Not just for salvation, like when I was seven. But to receive the inheritance of victory that is mine today. And after I receive him, he asks that I remain in him, like a trusting daughter refusing to leave her daddy's lap. Worship and service flow out in response from that safe, secure place of abiding in his presence. And even though there will be waves of temptation to keep the glory for myself or cower away in shame, and even though worry and anxiety will continue to scream at me when I am most vulnerable, the most important, life-changing thing this good girl can do is to remember to remember.

Remember you have a choice. Remember to let peace rule. Remember to believe God's truth even when it doesn't feel true. Remember that your life is hidden with Christ in God, you no longer have to manufacture your own safe places. And when we forget to remember? We don't have to travel over mountains and rough terrain to get back to God. Simply receive and believe that the truth is still true, and purpose to stay safely inside him.

> Now to Him who is able to do far more abundantly beyond all that we ask or think, according to the power that works within us, to Him be the glory in the church and in Christ Jesus to all generations forever and ever. Amen. (Eph. 3:20–21)

⟬ BEHIND THE MASK ⟭

In Psalm 139, David says that God has enclosed him behind and before. He says that God's hand has been laid upon him. As you lay your masks aside and stand vulnerably exposed, do you sense a desperate need to be enclosed? In what areas or circumstances of your life right now do you sense this need the most?

As you stand in that vulnerable place, ask yourself: What is the truth? What will I choose to believe? What will I choose to do? Will I give up the right to feel as if God's truth is true?

small group leader's guide

Hi there! I'm thankful and excited that you have chosen to study *Grace for the Good Girl* with your small group. As a recovering good girl in need of grace, it is my deepest prayer and desire to see women experience rescue from our incessant need to be good. We often move through life at top speed, longing to be valued for who we are but feeling most safe when we hide, hoping our try-hard life will make up for those places where we feel we lack. My prayer is that your small group of women will come out from their hiding places, release the lie of the try-hard life, and discover the beauty and freedom of a life hidden in Christ.

A Note to Leaders

Leading a small group of women can be a daunting task. Whether you are feeling qualified or unqualified, able or unable, prepared or unprepared, I understand. I know what it is to sit in the midst of a group of women who are looking to you to lead them. *What thoughts are lurking behind all those eyes? What are their fears, their hurts, and their expectations? And for the love of all things important, what are they thinking of me?!* I know what it is to feel inadequate and to quietly whisper inside your soul, *Lord, what were you thinking having me do this?!*

However, I also know there may be another side to leading a group, one that feels less needy. I know what it is to feel overly capable, to feel able, to believe I am qualified in my own strength because I know a thing or two about God, and to confidently whisper inside my soul *Lord, I've got this. I can take it from here.* Sometimes I feel both at the same time: feebly inadequate and arrogantly able. Can you relate or am I crazy?

Before you begin this time with your group, whether they are younger than you, older than you, or some mix of peers, I want to give you these verses that will be the basis upon which to build everything you do in your study:

> Such confidence we have through Christ toward God. Not that we are adequate in ourselves to consider anything as coming from ourselves, but our adequacy is from God, who also made us adequate as servants of a new covenant, not of the letter but of the Spirit; for the letter kills, but the Spirit gives life. (2 Cor. 3:4–6)

While I believe you were specifically chosen to lead this group, I want to gently remind you that you are adequate because God is. So whether you are feeling not-good-enough or comfortably adequate in yourself, the Lord knows and he is able. You are a servant of a new covenant—not a law-based, do-it-yourself kind of faith, but a grace-based, Jesus-already-did-it kind. This faith is based on his finished work, not our work yet to be done. So let me encourage you to lead from that place, a place of dependence, a place of freedom, a place of complete security. Thank you for being willing. May your time be a blessing, and may freedom ensue.

Confidentiality is key. This is the type of study that will get personal fast. Your group needs to feel safe. Encourage them to be honest about their experiences and assure them that their privacy will be protected.

Resist the urge to fix. As members begin to share ways in which they struggle, others may be tempted to try to "fix" or solve those problems. There also may be a tendency for members to justify one another's position, or to encourage others in their mask wearing. As the leader, and through the guidance of Jesus, encourage your group members to simply listen and ask questions as they discover things about themselves and one another. Too much advice giving could keep a person from recognizing the depravity of her flesh and may only encourage her to try harder, which is the exact opposite goal of this study.

Allow space for souls to breathe. Sometimes it's necessary to flounder in our own inadequacy for a bit before we realize our need for a Savior. That is what the first half of this study will do—turn the light on in the room of our souls to help us recognize the ways in which we hide and the futility of staying there. Remind everyone that they are not responsible to manufacture healing, either their own or anyone else's. Healing is a job that belongs to the Lord alone.

A word about the masks. Because I wrote the book, I can intimately relate with every mask listed. They are not my identity, but they are part of my story. That isn't to say that every good girl will relate with every mask here, and of course there are many other masks that we haven't explored. You and the women in your group may relate to only one or two of these false hiding places. Encourage them to be true to their own personalities. Don't try to pick up an issue that isn't yours.

Format

Part 1 *The Hiding*

Week 1: Introduction, Chapters 1–3
Week 2: Chapters 4–6

Week 3: Chapters 7–9
Week 4: Chapter 10

Part 2 *The Finding*

Week 5: Chapters 11–12
Week 6: Chapters 13–14

Part 3 *The Freedom of Being Found*

Week 7: Chapters 15–16
Week 8: Chapters 17–18

Length and Group Size: This study is designed to run for eight weeks, meeting once a week for approximately an hour and a half. It is discussion-heavy, so I would recommend your group be around six or less. As you will quickly discover, good girls have a lot to say when we finally get together and risk peeking out from our hiding places, so I would suggest meeting every week in order to encourage momentum and intimacy. Still, you may want to extend your time from eight weeks to ten in order to give more time for discussion.

Reading: The assigned reading for the week should be finished before the group meets. At your first meeting, your group will have read through chapter 3, for example.

Opening: The opening question will be an overall impression of that week's reading or a lighthearted thought to get you started. The purpose is simply to get a feel for what may have resonated that week.

Discuss Life behind the Mask: You will spend the bulk of your time here. While each chapter ends with several questions for the reader, you will not be expected to go over each of those questions during small group. You may want to begin your time by asking the women to share any questions or responses that may have been particularly meaningful to them. However, be aware of time here, as the questions provided in this guide will often overlap with the end-of-chapter questions.

Journal: Encourage each member to get a journal to record their responses to the Behind the Mask questions at the end of each chapter. Have them bring it to small group to use during the journaling time. Feel free to encourage your group to do their journal reflection at home if there isn't time to do so as a group.

Truth to Remember: Due to the introspective nature of this type of book, you will want to be sure and finish your time each week by encouraging your group to remember the truth that comes from God rather than staying stuck in the lies that sometimes come from our experience. You may even want to suggest they memorize the Truth to Remember verses, not to be graded or recited, but to practice hiding his Word in their hearts.

Song or Video Clip: In an attempt to provide options to you as the leader, each week there is either a suggested song to listen to or a video clip to watch together. Music and visual stories are sometimes able to communicate deep truths in ways simple words cannot.

are you a good girl in hiding?

hiding behind her performance and her good reputation

Read: Introduction, Chapters 1, 2, and 3

Video Clip: The masquerade scene from *The Phantom of the Opera* will provide a visual for the ways we tend to show our prettied-up versions to the world. A clip of this scene is available on YouTube if you enter "Masquerade Phantom of the Opera" into the search box. Or you can find the scene on the DVD, running from 1:17:20 until 1:20:00.

Opening Question: Let's begin by discussing your initial reaction to the concept of the "good girl" and see what impressions you may have about her. Can you think of any famous good girl characters in books, TV, or movies? (Examples: Monica from *Friends*, Diana from *Anne of Green Gables*, and Rory Gilmore from *Gilmore Girls*)

Discuss Life behind the Mask
Chapter 1 Are You a Good Girl in Hiding?

Take some time to share your stories with one another, especially identifying which brand of good girl you each might be. Did you accept Jesus as a child or as an adult? If you accepted Jesus as an adult, in what ways can you still relate with the good girl?

"She represented the girl I wanted to be but could never live up to."

- Discuss the presence of this good girl in your lives. When did she first show up?
- What does she look like, sound like, act like? When does she show up now?

There are unique ways good girls hide, ways that may be hard to discover because they are applauded by people we respect—pastors, teachers, and other good girls.

- Do you think of yourself as hiding?
- Do you agree that the best part of hiding is being found? Why or why not?

Chapter 2 Chasing Expectation: Hiding behind Her Good Performance

In the beginning of chapter 2, our twisted definitions of good are brought into the light. Finish this sentence as it relates to your current life stage: "Being good means that I . . ." (Example: *Being good means that I can handle everything.*)

Read Psalm 62:5—"My soul, wait only upon God and silently submit to Him; for my hope and expectation are from Him" (AMP).

- What does it mean for your hope and expectation to come from God alone?
- In what ways does the try-hard life fit into that verse?

Chapter 3 My Not-So-Extreme Makeover: Hiding behind Her Good Reputation

Sometimes it's easier to identify those experiences that wound us and cause some type of emotional scarring. We can point to those times as the beginning of a fear or insecurity, like when the boys at the basketball game made fun of my ears sticking out. But there are other words, *positive words*, that leave impressions on us, and they aren't always healthy impressions. Remember, children are the best recorders but the worst interpreters.

Instead of leaving a wound that causes the pain of rejection, positive words can leave a wound that awakens in us the pain of *perfection*. And this can be just as dangerous, because we don't see anything wrong with it.

- Invite the members of your group to identify any expectations that have left a wound causing them to experience the pain of perfection in their lives.

It's true that, as believers, we are called to a life set apart. But as good girls, we are often deceived about what that means and how to get there. Our good reputation becomes primary to everything else. Consider your current reputation. Remember, our reputation refers to how other people see us: the helpful volunteer, the pious single girl, the fun mom, or the one who can do everything.

- Can you identify ways in which you hide behind your good reputation?

Journal: Have the members of your group briefly write down their stories—the age when they accepted the Lord, the primary ways they've tried to live for him, and ways they believe they hide. Think list rather than novel. Use bullet points as things come to mind—this is a first impression type of exercise. As the weeks continue, this will hopefully become clearer. In what ways, if any, is your life telling a small story?

Truth to Remember: "God can do anything, you know—far more than you could ever imagine or guess or request in your wildest dreams! He does it not by pushing us around but by working within us, his Spirit deeply and gently within us" (Eph. 3:20 Message).

As the study continues, offer this reminder to your group: If you begin to feel "pushed around" by the knowledge of your own lack, that isn't the voice of God. He moves deeply and gently within us, not forcefully and rough without.

identify your hiding places

hiding behind her fake "fine," her servant heart, and her spiritual disciplines

Read: Chapters 4, 5, and 6

Opening: As a group, share your first impressions of the masks you read about in the chapters this week. In what ways, if any, do these masks resonate with you?

Discuss Life behind the Mask
Chapter 4 With a Wink and a Smile: Hiding behind Her Fake "Fine"
   Let's be honest about fine. It's true, there is a cultural surge of authenticity rolling through the church these days, causing "fine" to become less and less acceptable as an answer. But we still give it. We may not actually use the word, but good girls have a knack for creativity when it comes to deflecting questions and avoiding intimacy.

• What is your version of the fake fine?

- Do you tend to hide behind the fake fine out of fear, laziness, or some combination of both?

Chapter 5 Martha and My Many Things: Hiding behind Her Servant Heart

Martha is a great example of a good girl who did not hide behind a fake fine. She demanded of Jesus, "Tell her to help me!" She was not afraid to let people know when she was not fine. Martha's good girl struggle came from a different place, from the tension between pleasing God and trusting God.

- Can you identify ways in which your desire to please God has clouded your willingness to trust him?

Chapter 6 The Rule Follower: Hiding behind Her Spiritual Disciplines

While it can seem like there is a disregard for the law when we talk about grace, the opposite is actually true. Grace embraces the law, but only inasmuch as Jesus fulfilled it. And his Spirit lives within us. Jesus lived up to the law on our behalf! The law wasn't given for us to try to keep. It was given to show us we can't. Read this quote from Dudley Hall aloud to the group:

> Grace is not Jesus helping you live up to the law. This keeps us focused on the law. Jesus came to fulfill the law so we don't have to look at it anymore. I no more listen to what the law is saying, I listen to what Jesus is saying.

- What has been your relationship to the law in your life as a believer?
- In what ways could you relate with Lynne Hybels's fake Jesus on page 75?

Journal: Consider your thoughts on Mary in the account of Mary and Martha. Honestly record how you feel about her.

Perhaps you are miffed that it seems she got off easy, or maybe you are envious of her ability to shirk responsibility for the chance to worship. Last week in your journal, you recorded ways your life may be telling a small story. Have the women answer these questions in their journals:

What kind of story did Mary's life tell?
What about Martha's life?
In what ways is your life like the lives of these women?

Truth to Remember: "The former regulation is set aside because it was weak and useless (for the law made nothing perfect), and a better hope is introduced, by which we draw near to God" (Heb. 7:18–19 NIV).

Song: Ginny Owens, "True Story"

identify your hiding places

hiding behind her strength and responsibility, her comfort zone, and her indifference

Read: Chapters 7, 8, and 9

Opening: This week you explored the life of a good girl who hides behind her strength and responsibility, her comfort zone, and her indifference. Of those three masks, which one resonates most deeply with you? As you've now read all the hiding chapters, have you become more aware of the ways you hide in your everyday life?

Discuss Life behind the Mask
Chapter 7 Can't Fall Apart: Hiding behind Her Strength and Responsibility
    Reread Webster's definition of responsible: "liable to be called to account as the primary cause, motive, or agent."

- In what ways do you experience the weight of this kind of responsibility?
- Are you in the habit of teaching people you have no needs?
- How does it feel when they believe you?

Chapter 8 Picket Fences: Hiding behind Her Comfort Zone
Stepping out of our comfort zones doesn't necessarily mean doing daring or risky things. It doesn't always have to be so . . . *grand*. It may just be the difference between choosing the pencils or choosing the activity book, or considering what you really want to do rather than constantly weighing what you think everyone else wants.

- As a good girl, what keeps you from doing what you honestly want to do?
- When you consider choosing what your heart really desires, what emotions does that evoke? (Examples: afraid it is wrong or even sinful to do what we want to do; afraid it could be outside the will of God; afraid it is being selfish; afraid we might fail)

Chapter 9 When It Gets Ugly: Hiding behind Her Indifference
Remind the women in your group of the story of the two sons in Luke 15. Sometimes the bad girl stories seem more worthy of telling than ours. Both sons were completely accepted by the father, but the older son refused to go in to the party and celebrate. The older son was working to earn, similar to how good girls try to "live life for God."

- If your life has been one of rules rather than rebellion, do you ever feel as though God's grace is available to you only in a limited amount? That perhaps you don't get as much grace because you don't need it as much?
- What are some of the ways you "refuse to go in" and receive the abundance of grace that is offered?

Journal: Perhaps you are beginning to see that there is a life-sized difference between living a life *for* God and living a life *from* God. Take a few minutes and list every situation you can think of *that happened today* where you took responsibility for something that was out of your control. It could be feeling responsible for your husband's bad mood. Or it could be feeling overwhelmed by a responsibility to manage everyone's opinion of you or those close to you. Think about what it feels like to live that way, what emotions it brings to the surface.

- Is this what it also feels like to try to live for God?
- In what ways in your own life are you saying with the older brother, "I serve you and you never had a party for me!"

Truth to Remember: "Son, you have always been with me, and all that is mine is yours" (Luke 15:31).

Song: Sara Groves, "Different Kinds of Happy"

hide-and-seek

game over

Read: Chapter 10 and the part 2 introduction

Opening Question: This week, you only read one chapter and the part 2 introduction because there needed to be space to absorb some of these deep truths from Scripture. Take a few minutes to debrief with your group. Was there something in particular you read that has been rolling around in your mind and heart over the past few days?

Discuss Life behind the Mask

Your masks, or your flesh, will never completely go away. But we can learn what it looks and feels like to choose dependence on Jesus rather than dependence on self. There are many deep, spiritual truths to explore as we consider what it means to live life free of the masks we hide behind. Chapter 10 highlights five of them.

1. The two trees (Gen. 2:16–17). God put two trees in the Garden—the Tree of Life and the Tree of the Knowledge of

Good and Evil. You answered this question individually in your reading, so let's talk about it now as a group.

- Have you ever considered the fact that the forbidden tree was not just offering the knowledge of evil, but the knowledge of good as well?
- Why would God want to protect us from the knowledge of good?

2. The mask (or flesh) and the Spirit (Gal. 5:17). Take a few minutes to discuss which of the masks from chapters 2 through 9 each woman most personally identifies with. Perhaps there is one she can think of that isn't in the book.

- In what ways is living life from behind our masks similar to eating from the Tree of the Knowledge of Good and Evil? (Example: They are both a result of depending on ourselves to meet our own needs.)

3. Born into Adam vs. born into Christ (1 Cor. 15:21–22). Birth determines identity. This new birth is what provides the authority by which we can choose not to live behind the mask (our flesh). Because of the fall, every person is born into Adam—leading to death. But when we choose Jesus, we are reborn into Christ—leading to life.

- What does this say to you about the try-hard life?
- In what ways are you living your life as if you are still in Adam, that is, still eating from the Tree of Knowledge rather than the Tree of Life?

4. Guilt and shame. Guilt deals with our behavior while shame deals with our identity.

- Can you identify ways in which healthy conviction of sin could morph into unhealthy feelings of shame?

239

- How might this feed our attempts to be good girls living a try-hard life?

5. The mercy side of the cross and the grace side of the cross (Col. 1:13–14). God's mercy holds back the wrath we deserve—Jesus died in our place, offering forgiveness. God's grace lavishes upon us what we don't deserve—Jesus rose from the dead, offering life.

- If you live on the mercy side and avoid the grace side, of what will you constantly be aware? (Examples: the wrath you deserve, your need for forgiveness)
- When we embrace *both* sides of the cross, what is the result?
- Can you relate to being sure of your salvation but in desperate need of a rescue?
- What do you feel you most need to be rescued from? (Examples: impossible expectations, the weight of worry, the need to be liked, etc.)

Journal: We were created to hide, but not in a hiding place crafted by our own hands to get our needs met. We were made to find our safe place in God. Go back in your journal to week one where you briefly recorded some of the main points from your story. Which of these five truths did you least understand when you first accepted Jesus? Record in your own words how some of these truths are beginning to shape your story.

Truth to Remember: These masks, this girl-made hiding, are all a part of our flesh patterns. This may be how you cope, but this is not who you are. "For He rescued us from the domain of darkness, and transferred us to the kingdom of His beloved Son" (Col. 1:13).

Song: Matt Redman, "You Alone Can Rescue"

240

the finding

receive and *remain*

Read: Chapters 11 and 12

Movie Clip: If you have access to the movie, begin your time this week with a clip from *The Wizard of Oz,* the scene at the end where Glinda reveals to Dorothy that she's had the power to go home all along. You can find the scene on the DVD at 1:33:44 until 1:39:10.

Opening Question: Dorothy and her friends in *The Wizard of Oz* are a great example of a group of people who needlessly lived the try-hard life. They already had what they were looking for, they just didn't know how to let it be true. In what ways could you relate with the concept of working hard for something you've already been given?

Discussion from behind the Mask
Chapter 11 Receive: On Truth and Trusting
    Read 1 Thessalonians 5:23—"Now may the God of peace Himself sanctify you entirely; and may your spirit and soul

and body be preserved complete, without blame at the coming of our Lord Jesus Christ." Discuss with your group the differences between the soul and the spirit.

Body: our five senses; what people can see and touch—our way of relating with our environment

Soul: our mind (thoughts), our emotions (feelings), and our will (decision-making)—our way of relating with other people

Spirit: our inner man, our true self, our identity—our way of relating with God

- Does understanding the difference between soul and spirit change the way you think about being a good girl? Why or why not?
- What keeps you from receiving "every spiritual blessing in Christ" as promised in Ephesians 1?

Chapter 12 Remain: On Quiet and Time
In Exodus 3, Moses made the shift from asking *Who am I?* to considering *Who is I AM?*

- What is important about this shift?
- Share with one another your experiences of having a quiet time.
- Is there something in your life that has led to a deepening in the way you approach time with the Lord of the Universe?

Journal: Refer to Galatians 5:22–23, which lists the fruit of the Spirit. Write each one down in your journal. Circle the ones that are the most difficult for you to let be true in your life. **This is not so you can "work on those fruits" to get better at them.** Rather, it is intended to make you aware of all the gifts that are available to you, so you can ask the Lord to enable

242

you to let these gifts that you already have become evident in your life. At the bottom of your list, write down Galatians 5:25: "If we live by the Spirit, let us also walk by the Spirit." These things are already true of you in your spirit. As you depend on Jesus, he will bring out the evidence in your life.

Truth to Remember: "Let the peace of Christ rule in your hearts, to which indeed you were called in one body; and be thankful. Let the word of Christ richly dwell within you" (Col. 3:15–16a).

Video: For a great example of "Christ in you," visit http://www.youtube.com/watch?v=bYI_aOyCn9Y&feature=player _embedded

the finding

respond and *remember*

Read: Chapters 13 and 14

Opening Question: This week you read about worship, service, and setting your minds. Do you have any new impressions of what it means to worship and serve?

Discussion from behind the Mask
Chapter 13 Respond: On Worship and Service

- Do you tend to see worship and service as one of the slices on your life's pie chart?
- How does being a good girl influence the way you divide up life?
- Read Luke 1:46–55. What can we learn about worship and service from Mary?

Chapter 14 Remember: On Setting Your Mind
   To act differently we must think differently. We need to discover new patterns of belief. If we don't set our minds,

they will set themselves, just like the screen saver on the computer. Ask the women if anyone would like to share what their mind's default screen saver is. (Examples: worry, fear, anger, shame)

Read Romans 8:6—"For the mind set on the flesh is death, but the mind set on the Spirit is life and peace." Brainstorm with one another what it looks like to set your mind on the Spirit when your mind automatically goes to your screen saver.

Journal: Take a few minutes to list all the roles you play in life: friend, mother, daughter, wife, teacher, etc. If you are caught up in the try-hard life, perhaps you are accustomed to mustering up the strength to accomplish the tasks required of you. Take some time this week to surrender each of these roles into the hands of your loving, capable God. Receive your abilities from him and release your inabilities to him. *This is your spiritual act of worship.*

Truth to Remember: "Set your mind on the things above, not on the things that are on earth. For you have died and your life is hidden with Christ in God" (Col. 3:2–3).

Song: Fernando Ortega, "Give Me Jesus"

the freedom of being found

safe, even when it hurts and *safe, even in failure*

Read: Part 3 Introduction, chapters 15 and 16

Opening Question: What type of systems have you created in order to finish tasks? Do you cross through items, fill in boxes, or check things off?

Discussion from behind the Mask
Chapter 15 Safe, Even When It Hurts
   As a group, discuss the difference between closure and healing. In John 12, Jesus predicts his death when he says, "Truly, truly, I say to you, unless a grain of wheat falls into the earth and dies, it remains alone; but if it dies, it bears much fruit."

- What is the role of brokenness in the healing process?
- What is the fruit that comes from falling to the ground?

Chapter 16 Safe, Even in Failure
   Ask the women in your group what comes to mind when they hear the word "failure." Good girls tend to think of

failure as not measuring up, or of doing or being wrong. Perhaps God's perspective of failure is simply our unwillingness to depend on him.

- In what ways might this definition of failure frustrate the mask-wearing good girl?
- What does dependence on Jesus look like as we are affected by the failures of others?

Journal: Write down all the rights you may be holding on to. For example, your right to be understood, your right to find a spouse, your right to feel appreciated. Consider spending some time in prayer as you bring this list out into the open, and honestly answer this question: *Would you rather be right or live free?* When you have some time alone, speak these rights out loud and release them to Jesus. For example, if one of the rights you cling to is the right to a good reputation, your prayer may sound something like this: *Lord, I release my right to manage other people's opinions of me. I receive your acceptance and trust you to meet my needs.*

Truth to Remember: "Have this attitude in yourselves which was also in Christ Jesus, who, although He existed in the form of God, did not regard equality with God a thing to be grasped, but emptied Himself, taking the form of a bondservant, and being made in the likeness of men" (Phil. 2:5–7).

Song: Tenth Avenue North, "Healing Begins"

the freedom of being found

safe, even when it all goes wrong and *safe, even when you don't feel safe*

Read: Chapters 17 and 18

Opening Question: Feelings can be an inaccurate measure of reality. Ask if anyone has a story to share of a time when they felt unsafe when, in fact, they were very safe. Or perhaps someone can remember a time when they felt safe but were, in fact, in danger.

Discussion from behind the Mask
Chapter 17 Safe, Even When It All Goes Wrong
    Discuss your answer to the following question: What is the difference between *things going right* and *things working together for good*? Does Romans 8:28 and 31–32 provide any insight to your answers?

> Enjoy the tempo of a God-breathed life by letting him set the pace.
>
> —Sarah Young, *Jesus Calling*

- What does it look like for you to live in the rhythm of a God-breathed life?
- What are some ways that our good-girl-ness makes it difficult to receive that tempo?

Chapter 18 Safe, Even When You Don't Feel Safe

At the end of chapter 18, you were introduced to a series of questions to ask when you find yourself in a situation where your safety seems to be challenged:

What is the truth?
What will I choose to believe?
What will I choose to do?
Will I give up the right to feel as if this is true?

Share your impressions of these questions with one another. They are not meant to be formulaic; rather, they are a practical tool to bring out the truth that God has already placed in our hearts. Is there a situation recently where you have felt unsafe? Ask if anyone is willing to share their answers to these questions as they apply to situations in their lives.

Journal: The Lord is building a track record of his own faithfulness into your life. As you receive the lovely, the messy, and the unexpected as daily graces from his hand, you will have something to refer to when things go wrong and when the truth doesn't feel true. Start today. In the time you have, record all the gifts the Lord has delivered just today. Write down evidences of your safety as you ask God to reveal them to you.

Truth to Remember: "You have enclosed me behind and before, and laid Your hand upon me" (Ps. 139:5).

Song: Phil Wickham, "Safe"

in conclusion . . .

Can we really let go of this try-hard life? In the middle of a Tuesday when the everyday mundane seems to be the only reality there is, when our feelings swirl and hint and whisper that our to-do list is unmanageable and there is no escape from this treadmill called life, when the doctor calls you in because the tests came back and it doesn't look good, *we are able to pause*. Because of our new life in Christ, we have access to a source outside of ourselves, a Person who can handle it, a limitless supply of grace, peace, and overwhelming love. We belong to another, we are safe in his presence, we are dearly loved, and we can rest.

Video: As a fun way to end, Google "T-Mobile dance" or "Sound of Music flash mob" to show at your final meeting.

According to Wikipedia, a flash mob is "a large group of people who assemble suddenly in a public place, perform an unusual and pointless act for a brief time, then disperse." But these examples are, to me, anything but pointless. Their message is one word: *joy*. What a beautiful, fun example of what we can experience as we come out of hiding, let go of the try-hard life, and embrace the mystery of "Christ in you, the hope of glory."

And also? It's contagious.

notes

Chapter 1 Are You a Good Girl in Hiding?

1. Biblos, s.v. "Genesis 1:4," accessed July 12, 2010, http://biblos.com/genesis/1–4.htm.

2. Biblos, s.v. "3966. Meod," accessed July 12, 2010, http://strongsnumbers.com/hebrew/3966.htm.

Chapter 2 Chasing Expectation

1. Bill Thrall, Bruce McNicol, and John Lynch, *TrueFaced* (Colorado Springs: NavPress, 2004), 24.

Chapter 3 My Not-So-Extreme Makeover

1. David Seamands, *Healing for Damaged Emotions* (Colorado Springs: Chariot Victor, 1991), 69.

2. Fil Anderson, *Breaking the Rules* (Downers Grove, IL: InterVarsity Press, 2010), 47.

Chapter 4 With a Wink and a Smile

1. Sara, November 21, 2009 (1:52 a.m.), comment on Emily Freeman, "Picket Fences," November 19, 2009, *Chatting at the Sky* (blog), http://www.chattingatthesky.com.

2. Holley Gerth, "I Cried on the Way to Panera Café This Morning," *Heart to Heart with Holley* (blog), March 1, 2009, http://blog.dayspring.com/2009/03/i-cried-on-the-way-to-panera-café-this-morning.html.

3. Holley Gerth, "A Different Kind of Hope: Part One," *Heart to Heart with Holley*, December 10, 2009, http://blog.dayspring.com/2009/12/a-different-kind-of-hope-part-one.html.

4. Tammy Maltby, *Confessions of a Good Christian Girl* (Nashville: Thomas Nelson, 2007), 15.

5. "The Beauty Contest," *Designing Women,* CBS. Original air date October 6, 1986. http://www.imdb.com/title/tt0090418/quotes.

6. Dan Stone and Greg Smith, *The Rest of the Gospel* (Dallas: One Press, 2000), 71–72.

7. Ibid.

Chapter 5 Martha and My Many Things

1. Major Ian Thomas, *The Indwelling Life of Christ* (Colorado Springs: Multnomah, 2006), 69.

2. Thrall, McNicol, and Lynch, *TrueFaced,* 37.

3. Renee Swope, *A Confident Heart* (Grand Rapids: Revell, 2011).

Chapter 6 The Rule Follower

1. Dudley Hall, *Grace,* sound recording, Successful Christian Living Ministries, Euless, TX, 1991. http://www.sclm.org/

2. Lynne Hybels, *Nice Girls Don't Change the World* (Grand Rapids: Zondervan, 2005), 30–31.

3. Hall, "Grace."

Chapter 7 Can't Fall Apart

1. Merriam-Webster Online, s.v. "responsible," accessed July 15, 2010, http://www.merriam-webster.com/dictionary/responsible.

2. Kelly Langner Sauer, "Love Stories: The Purse—Part 1," *This Restless Heart* (blog), March 2010, http://www.kellylangnersauer.com/blog/2010/03/25/love-stories-the-purse-part-i/.

Chapter 8 Picket Fences

1. From comments on Emily Freeman, "Choose Life," *(in)courage* (blog), March 8, 2010, http://www.incourage.me/2010/03/choose-the-pencils-choose-to-live.html.

Chapter 9 When It Gets Ugly

1. Brennan Manning, *Reflections for Ragamuffins*, 1st ed. (New York: HarperSanFrancisco, 1998), 317.

Chapter 10 Hide-and-Seek

1. Dudley Hall, *Grace Works* (Ann Arbor, MI: Vine Books, 1992), 164.
2. Dan Stone and Greg Smith, *The Rest of the Gospel* (Dallas: One Press, 2002), 42–43.

Chapter 11 Receive

1. A.D.A.M, s.v. "Skeletal System," accessed April 13, 2010, www.best health.com/besthealth/bodyguide/reftext/html/skel_sys_fin.html#bone.
2. Biblos, s.v. "Colossians 3:15," accessed April 22, 2010, http://bible lexicon.org/colossians/3–15.htm.
3. Merriam-Webster Online, s.v. "umpire," accessed April 22, 2010, http://www.merriam-webster.com/dictionary/umpire.
4. Malcolm Smith, *Let God Love You: The Answer to Your Every Longing Begins with Love* (Tulsa, OK: Harrison House, 2003), 10.

Chapter 12 Remain

1. Sarah Young, *Jesus Calling: A 365-Day Journaling Devotional* (Nashville: Thomas Nelson, 2010), 41.
2. Biblos, s.v. "1774. Enoikeo," accessed July 9, 2010, http://strongs numbers.com/greek/1774.htm.
3. Kenneth S. Wuest, *Ephesians and Colossians in the Greek New Testament* (Grand Rapids: Eerdmans, 1954), 226–27.

Chapter 16 Safe, Even in Failure

1. Presten Gillham, *Grace in Ungracious Places*, Association of Exchanged Life Ministries National Convention, April 26, 2002.
2. "The Evidence of Brokenness," Association of Exchanged Life Ministries workbook (Aurora: Cross Life, 1998), 28.
3. Biblos, s.v. "725. Harpagmos," accessed July 17, 2010, http://strongs numbers.com/greek/725.htm; ibid., s.v. "726. harpazo," accessed July 17, 2010, http://strongsnumbers.com/greek/726.htm.

Chapter 17 Safe, Even When It All Goes Wrong

1. Heather George, "Emma's Story," *Especially Heather* (blog), no date, accessed March 15, 2010, http://especiallyheather.com/emma/.
2. Heather George, "The Cancer," *Especially Heather*, no date, accessed March 15, 2010, http://especiallyheather.com/the-cancer/.
3. Heather George, "Oh My God, I Have a Brain Tumor!" *Especially Heather*, April 12, 2007, http://especiallyheather.com/2007/04/12/oh-my-god-i-have-a-brain-tumor/.

4. Holley Gerth, "A Different Kind of Hope: Part Five," *Heart to Heart with Holley*, December 17, 2009, http://blog.dayspring.com/2009/12/a-different-kind-of-hope-part-five.html.

5. Larry Crabb, *The Pressure's Off* (Colorado Springs: Waterbrook, 2002), 64–65.

6. Young, *Jesus Calling*, 26.

7. Heather George, "Good Things," *Especially Heather*, May 17, 2010, http://especiallyheather.com/2010/05/17/good-things/.

NOTE: Emma finally received her full healing in the arms of Jesus on April 22, 2011. Heather continues to believe God even as she misses her sweet Emma.

Chapter 18 Safe, Even When You Don't Feel Safe

1. Four questions from a talk by Lee Whitman and Dale Dunnewald, GraceLife Conference, March 2003, Westover Church, Greensboro, NC.

acknowledgments

*I*t's hard for a good girl to come up with the courage to write a whole book. There are way too many people to potentially disappoint, and you know how much she fears that. That fear nearly stopped me from taking on this message, as it would have been much safer to stay hidden under my coffee table. What you hold in your beautiful hands is proof that the God who created the heavens and the earth with words alone continues to create with words through us. He has rescued me from the control of fear. So when he said, *Write*, I said, *Okay*. Thank you, Lord Jesus, for saving my life.

And thank you to the multitude of friends, mentors, and family who have poured out grace upon grace:

To my husband, John—You are a living example of grace for this recovering good girl. My story would not have been complete or possible without you. You show me on a daily basis what it means to love, and you pour out acceptance over me without inhibition. I am always proud to stand next to you, and I have a life-size crush on you.

And to Ava, Stella, and Luke—You are our most important, cherished, and loved work of art. May my story shape yours in a good way. And if not, I promise to pay your counseling bills.

To Mom—Even though I was a ball of perfectionistic anxiety when I was a kid when "I didn't know how to do first grade," you were patient and kind and never got mad at my irrational fears.

And to Dad—You showed me with your life what it means to depend on Jesus. We are all so thankful for your wisdom, support, and love. You are a living miracle.

To my other parents, Sherry and Frank—Your acceptance of and love for me is overwhelming in so many ways. I am honored and blessed to be in your family.

To my college roommate, Faith Gragg Roehm—You taught me what it means to be grace-filled long before I was ready to receive it.

To my dear friend, Kendra Adachi—Without your support, this book would never have been written. Thank you for those words you said that cold December day, coffee between us, fear all over my face. Your encouragement helped to set me free to write this message.

To my friend and counselor, Steve Lynam—Your fingerprints are woven throughout this book, the beauty of Christ's life poured out through your unique personality. A heartfelt thank you seems too small.

To Don and Donna Miller and the people of Westover Church—It is a joy to be part of a church where the gospel of grace is taught, embraced, and lived out.

To my girlfriends who read choppy chapters at various stages—Sissy, Vicky, Stacey, Melissa, Kari, Katherine, Sarah, Katie, and Dianne—your friendship, stories, and encouragement came at just the right time.

To Bonita Lillie—You were able to see beauty in my messy book proposal and were willing to stand with me in the muck of it. You inspire courage in me.

To Lysa TerKeurst—You are brave and your courage fills the room, and somehow a little of it rubbed off on me. Thank you for telling me to *write that book*.

To my editor at Revell, Andrea Doering, because you are a good girl too, and you were willing to take a chance on me. And to the entire Revell team, Twila, Janelle, Cheryl, Amy, Barb, and so many others—you never made me feel like the rookie I am. You made this book sing.

To the readers of Chatting at the Sky and the community of women at (in)courage who have become real life friends, because without your kind words, prayers, and emails to remind me why I do what I do, I would never have been the least bit productive and would have wasted all my time browsing Etsy and People.com.

And even though I don't know you in person, thank you, Ingrid Michaelson and Jon Foreman, because without your music in my earbuds, I would have surely lost all inspiration while writing in that dark corner of the coffee shop.

And to you. Thank you, my fellow recovering good girl. I am humbled down into a puddle to imagine you sitting there with my words in your hands. It is the most beautiful gift to have the privilege of sharing my story with you, to have you turn these pages, to imagine you sharing these words with one another. Let's dare to let go of the try-hard life together.

Emily Freeman is a writer who loves to read and a speaker who would rather listen. She writes for DaySpring (a division of Hallmark) and has also traveled as a writer with Compassion International to raise awareness for the needs of children in poverty around the world. She attended Columbia International University to study the Bible and the University of North Carolina at Greensboro where she earned a degree in Educational Interpreting for the Deaf. She is married to John, a student ministries pastor, and together they live in North Carolina with their three children. Emily extends a daily invitation on her blog for women to create space for their souls to breathe. Come join the community of grace dwellers at www.ChattingAtTheSky.com.

Dear Friend,

I imagine you sitting there in your comfy spot, holding this book and reading these words. Perhaps you read them alone or maybe you share them with a small group of women. Either way, I hope you have seen in these pages the art, beauty, and freedom of being found. If so, I would love to hear from you.

Jesus didn't come so we could fret and worry our way through life as good girls. He didn't come to push us around through fear, *He came to lead us in love.* If you would like to receive some daily encouragement to remember the truth, join me and a most beautiful community of friends at Chatting at the Sky as we embrace the messy beauty and daily release our tight grip on this try-hard life.

Found and thankful.

Emily

blog: *www.ChattingAtTheSky.com*
contact: *www.chattingatthesky.com/contact*

Through stunning photos and honest words, Emily offers a daily dose of grace and creativity on her blog. Come join the community of grace dwellers at www.ChattingAtTheSky.com and click on "subscribe" to have new posts delivered for free right into your email inbox.